SUCCESSFUL
TRAPPING METHODS

A GUIDE TO GOOD TRAPPING
Second Edition

by

WALTER S. CHANSLER
Author of *The River Trapper*

WITH NUMEROUS SKETCHES BY THE AUTHOR

VNR **VAN NOSTRAND REINHOLD COMPANY**
New York   Cincinnati   Toronto   London   Melbourne

Published by Van Nostrand Reinhold Company
A division of Litton Educational Publishing, Inc.
135 West 50th Street, New York, N.Y. 10020

Van Nostrand Reinhold Limited
1410 Birchmount Road
Scarborough, Ontario MIP 2E7, Canada

Van Nostrand Reinhold Australia Pty. Ltd.
17 Queen Street
Mitcham, Victoria 3132, Australia

Van Nostrand Reinhold Company Limited
Molly Millars Lane
Wokingham, Berkshire, England

Preface

With the aim of making the information in this book as widely useful as possible, the author has ever kept in mind the needs of trappers everywhere in all ranks of proficiency. He has endeavored to set forth in this volume such information as will be helpful to the youngsters who have never set traps, but who would like to try their hands at trapping for fur game; to the youthful trappers who have done some little trapping, but who are still confused about the "ways and means" of taking fur-bearing animals in steel traps; to the older trappers who spend some of their spare time in winter at trapping in the settled districts; and to the professional trappers who, because of their keen understanding of the necessity of acquiring that peculiar skill and deftness that lead to good trapping, know the value to them of the other fellow's experiences in trapping fur game. For all such persons, the book has been planned and executed.

Besides the several chapters on the various aspects of trapping in general, the book contains much information on the characteristics and habits of many of the fur-bearing animals, as well as no little enlightenment on how to prepare traps and set them for successfully capturing most kinds of animals in this class. There are chapters on such subjects as locating trapping grounds, finding signs and tracks of fur game, selecting equipment, laying out the trap line, the use of trapping devices, trapping tricks and aids, finding set locations, making sets, skinning fur game and caring for raw furs, tanning fur skins, and laws that affect trapping. Other chapters deal with such points as how and where to trap for the many species of fur-bearing animals, together with advice on skinning, stretching, and valuing the pelts.

A few words in these prefatory notes about conserving wild animal life may not be out of place, since all good trappers are, or should want to be, good conservationists. Although this book was written primarily for the purpose of aiding the trapping fraternity to catch more fur-bearing animals and to do it with greater ease and certainty, it would grieve the writer's heart sorely to know that even one reader might use any of the information therein to enable him to trap the last animal of any species from his trapping grounds. The good trapper will always leave plenty of animals for seed for the next crop. This is only good business. In no other way can we insure good trapping in the years to come.

We should never destroy dens, trap too late in the season, trap early in the fall, nor use poison to kill fur game. Destroying dens leaves fur-bearing animals without homing places to rear their young. Late spring trapping interferes with the mating of the fur-bearers and kills off many females that may be carrying young. Early fall trapping results in the taking of many young animals the skins of which have no great value in raw fur markets. And the use of poison, while unlawful in many sections, often kills animals that are never found. Poisoning may be a menace to fur game for many months after the trapping season has legally closed.

Let us keep in mind the fact that a good trapper always gives the wild animals an even break, catching his share only when the skins are full-furred and prime.

WALTER S. CHANSLER

Contents

v

Chapter I

The Trapping Grounds

Trapping and fur-trading are two of our oldest vocations. It was the buckskin-clad trapper and the bold fur-trader who in early days pushed westward over the mountains from the handful of scattered settlements along the Atlantic Coast to claim that vast wilderness which lay beyond, stretching away for more than two thousand miles toward the setting sun. Braving hardships and defying death, these intrepid adventurers plied their vocations among dangerous wild animals and hostile Indians, blazing trails for the unique civilization that was to follow them. In fact, they were the real explorers of this great land of ours, the advance guard that opened the way for the early settlers.

Penetrating every section of this great wilderness—from the frozen tundra of the far North to the swamps of the Mississippi Delta country, and from the heavily forested Alleghanies to the distant Pacific Coast—these rugged men of the woods and wild places lived in daily peril, often alone, with only the simplest necessities of life. Traveling by sled or on snowshoes in the north-

1

ern sections, by birch-bark canoes of their own making in the forested areas where there were lakes and streams, and on horseback in the Southwest and West, they tended trap lines and collected fur skins from the Indians, often being away from the settlements for several months at a time. They made their own deadfalls and snares, procured their food supplies mostly from day to day, made their own clothing from the skins of wild animals, molded their own rifle balls, and depended upon flint and steel for fire. It is to these daring adventurers more than to any other type of pioneer that this nation owes undying gratitude for its early exploration and development.

TRAPPING GROUNDS OF EARLY DAYS

The early pioneer in this country was never at a loss to find good trapping. In fact, he lived in the very midst of trapping grounds that were unequaled anywhere in the world. The dense and almost trackless forest that surrounded his crude log cabin was teeming with all sorts of fur-bearing animals, from the dangerous grizzly bear to the lowly musquash or muskrat. European markets had created a great demand for the skins of these animals; and it was with delight that the pioneer trapper found that he could swap his beaver skins and 'coon pelts at almost any settlement for much of what he needed in the way of supplies. So he trapped the wilderness for the animal pelts that would get him powder and bullets, hunting knives, and the few necessities he required for his work in the woods.

Thus he pushed on deeper and deeper into the wilderness, ever westward, where virgin trapping territory beckoned—through trackless forests, on lakes and streams, across wide prairies, in rugged mountain regions, wherever the signs of fur-bearing animals lead him to believe there would be good trapping. He visited and explored such rivers as the Ohio, the Mississippi, the Missouri; and farther west, beyond the Great Plains, the Colorado and the Columbia. He penetrated deserts, climbed formidable mountain ranges, pushed across sagebrush-choked plateaus, and camped on wide, illimitable prairies. Wherever fur-bearers were found in plenty, there were his trapping grounds.

Certain sections of this vast wilderness, however, were favored by trappers because of the fine quality of the fur of some of the fur-bearing animals found there. Thus, beaver trappers were anxious to locate in the Great Lakes region or in the far Northwest;

mink and raccoon trappers turned toward the heavily wooded streams of the Mississippi Basin; bear hunters and trappers worked the foothills of the Rocky Mountains, and, farther west, the rugged slopes of the Cascade and the Sierra Nevada mountains; while muskrat trappers gravitated either to the Great Lakes region or farther south to the Mississippi Delta country.

Although the old-time trapper worked under many hardships and difficulties, he nevertheless had one big advantage over his modern counterpart; he had only to enter the heavily forested areas almost anywhere to find an abundance of fur-bearing animals. He had all sorts of wilderness terrain from which to choose a trapping ground. He could trap the lakes, bayous, rivers, and small tributary streams by canoe; he could tend a long line of traps in the prairie country on horseback; if he wished, he might establish a long trap line in mountainous regions for marten, visiting the traps on snowshoes; or he might put out a long line of traps in any forested area, using a main camp together with many overnight camps. He could be fairly certain of good catches wherever he trapped; and he seldom needed to worry about trap thieves or fur pilferers.

WILDERNESS SECTIONS OF TODAY

Of course most of the true wilderness sections in the United States have long ago been transformed into comparatively well-settled ranching and farming districts. Where the howl of the wolf and the cries of all sorts of wild animals used to disturb the sleep of the lonely, weary trapper, now is heard the chug of the tractor and the rattle of the combine, as farmers reap the harvests of golden grain. Only in widely scattered areas are there a few isolated spots where bits of the old-time wilderness may yet be found. Most of these occur in sections where there are mountains, swamps, deserts, or where other hindrances have prevented the settling of the country by ranchers or farmers.

The few sections of wilderness country to be found today anywhere in the United States lie in Maine, New York, South Carolina, Michigan, Oklahoma, Minnesota, Wyoming, Arizona, New Mexico, Washington, Oregon, and northern California. Farther north, the provinces of Canada have some extensive tracts of wild country. These appear in British Columbia, Saskatchewan, New Ontario, Alberta, and Manitoba. There are vast forested areas in some parts of Quebec, and wild areas of no little extent over most of the northern part of Canada.

Nowhere on the North American continent will one find wilderness sections comparable with those found in the eastern and western parts of the United States back when the Indians were in full possession of the country. For one thing, the larger game animals and the more valuable fur-bearing animals have been so reduced in numbers that they now appear in plenty in only a very, very few remote spots, where man for one reason or another has not seen fit to settle. Another reason is, the drainage of swamps and the cutting of forests incident to the development of agriculture have so depleted the natural habitats of many of the game and fur-bearing animals that they have been unable to live and multiply as they formerly did. Pasturing, too, has had its effect, particularly in the Great Plains region and among the foothills of the Rocky Mountains. Only those species of game and fur-bearing animals that can well adapt themselves to the changes brought about by the progress of an advancing civilization have survived and may yet be found in fairly plentiful numbers in some of the more settled districts.

BEST TRAPPING GROUNDS

There is an old saying to the effect that the grass always seems greenest on the other side of the fence. Applying this to trapping, we might say that the trapping grounds in some far-off country always seem to offer better possibilities than those found in our own home territory. In the judgment of many trappers, this would seem to be true. For it appears that a great many trappers see all the encouraging features of the trapping ground away off yonder, but overlook the wonderful opportunities to be had in trapping the back pastures and creek bottoms near home.

Everywhere throughout this broad land of ours, trappers are dissatisfied with their surroundings. With his traps buried beneath three feet of snow, the long-line trapper of the far north countries sits moodily before the red-hot stove in his crude home cabin, longing for the joys of trapping in more southern climes, where fur-bearing animals are plentiful and the thermometer seldom registers below zero. The muskrat trapper in the swamps of Louisiana wants to try trapping in Alaska. The farm youth, tending a few traps along the creek near his home, thinks of the wonderful catches that might be his if he were on a distant trap line in the mountains or at a good location along some wilderness lake shore. And so it goes. But a trapper's trapping abilities are often more important than

the location of his trapping grounds. A good trapper in poor territory will often catch more fur game than a poor trapper in good
territory. Anyway, trappers will do well to learn to trap the common, easily captured fur-bearers near their homes before giving too
much thought to trying for the crafty and more wary animals 'way
off yonder in some wilderness country.

The best trapping grounds, of course, are those where one can
catch the most fur game with the least effort. Usually such locations
will be found near home, more frequently in a part of the country
with which one is most familiar. These spots, which almost never
are very large, are known as "fur pockets." They are spots that have
been overlooked or otherwise passed up by local trappers for a few
years. This has enabled the fur game there to multiply and restock
itself. Such spots are found in nearly all parts of the country. Any
energetic trapper may be able to locate one or more of these, if he
will only spend enough time in looking about his grounds, visiting
the more inaccessible and secluded places.

What Makes Trapping Grounds Good

What does one look for when prospecting a locality with the view
of trapping there? Tracks, dens, trails, and feeding grounds of
the fur-bearers one expects to catch? Yes—and more! One must
find good set locations—plenty of them. It is entirely possible to
catch mink by making a set where the animals have been using
along the edge of a bare sandbar. But how much easier it is to
catch them at drifts, root wads, springs, and in trails under overhanging banks! Plenty of suitable set locations are necessary to
make any trapping grounds good.

Other features of the trapping grounds that one will do well to
consider are those of terrain and cover. Good trapping is usually
found in sections where there are brushy woods bordering lakes and
streams, hills, rocky canyons, springs, thickets, swamps, and the like.
Places like these usually have plenty of good set locations and are
fairly well stocked with fur game. An abundance of the natural
foods of fur-bearing animals, too, is another prerequisite of good
trapping. No matter how well a trapping ground may be supplied
with cover, or how favorable its terrain, if it does not produce an
abundance of natural foods for wildlife, it will not have fur-bearing
animals in sufficient numbers to make it a good place to trap.

So in looking for good trapping grounds, notice particularly the
nature of the terrain and cover of the tract under consideration.

See if there are plenty of good set locations; and observe especially how well they are distributed over the area. Look for the natural food supply of the kinds of animals that are to be found there; and locate, if possible, some of the feeding grounds. Then prospect the area for dens, signs, tracks, trails, and runways; and do enough snooping about to become thoroughly familiar with every acre of the tract. For no matter how good the trapping prospects of a given place may be, one's trapping success there will likely not be at all spectacular unless one has become thoroughly familiar with all parts of the area.

Chapter II

Finding Good Trapping

Usually the first thought that occurs to us when we are in need of work is that we must get out and look for a job. We know that if we do not look for work, it will not come to us, unsought. There may be opportunity for work on an adjoining lot or on a neighboring farm; but if we do not look about us and find the opening, we will never know anything about it. It is much the same in trapping. One may be in the very midst of good trapping opportunities and yet be utterly unaware of it. Only by getting out in the woods and along the streams for the purpose of looking up signs of fur game and trying to locate good set locations can one form any idea of the sort of trapping that may be possible in any given territory.

Good trapping, like good farming or good salesmanship, usually stems from thorough preparation. The trapper who consistently makes good catches day after day has without doubt spent a lot of time on his trapping grounds before the opening of the season in studying tracks, trails, and signs, and in looking up dens and feeding grounds, as well as in locating the haunts of the fur-bearers that are using in that locality. He has undoubtedly become thoroughly familiar with every acre of the area; knows where the animals are denning, traveling, and feeding; and has spent no little time in looking everywhere for good places to set his traps. He knows that he must acquire this knowledge before he can reasonably expect to do good trapping in that locality.

Where to Look for Good Trapping

Like gold, good trapping is where you find it. However, there are certain features in any given area that indicate whether or not one is likely to find good trapping there. Experienced trappers are ever on the watch for these features; inexperienced trappers often fail to give them much attention.

Sections that are well drained by a number of little, crooked, bush-fringed streams that come down from partly wooded hills where there are rocky cliffs usually offer good trapping for skunk, fox, or raccoon, provided they appear in a part of the country inhabited by these fur-bearers. Likewise, swamps, marshes, lakes, rivers, and small streams often are good places for trapping muskrat, otter, and mink. Rocky arroyos choked with sagebrush, canyons, and sandy, cacti-grown areas in Western sections are good places to trap for wolf and coyote. Forested areas high in the mountains often offer good marten trapping. And open farming country interspersed with much waste land, many thickets, and an occasional bit of woodland can hardly be beaten for trapping opossum. By carefully observing the terrain in any locality, the experienced trapper can often form a pretty good idea of the kinds of fur game to be found there, as well as to make a fair estimate of its plentifulness or scarcity.

Any locality will often have spots that offer unusual opportunities for trapping fur game. These may be places in thickets where a number of game trails cross; they may be at overhanging banks along a stream, where there are a number of mink or muskrat dens; they may be found around waterholes, or at or near springs; they may be at places where trails cut across big bends in a stream, or where a log spans a creek. All such places are worth the notice of the trapper who wants to make the most of his opportunities. Some trapping grounds have many such spots; others have only a few at widely scattered places. But it will well pay any trapper to keep alert to the opportunities offered by such places, and to watch for them when prospecting any locality.

Few trappers ever think about the opportunities for trapping that exist near towns and cities. However, I know several trappers who are doing well trapping in the outlying districts near towns, and even near big cities. I, myself, once prospected along a small stream at the outskirts of a city of some 400,000 inhabitants and found many signs of fur game—skunks, minks, raccoons, and muskrats. Also, an expert trapper once told me that the best trapping he had ever experienced came not from wild forested areas, but from areas near large cities, such as Detroit, Michigan, Pittsburgh, Pennsylvania, St. Louis, Missouri, and Washington, D.C. He had been trapping localities such as these for years. Good trapping may often be had in many unsuspected places.

GOOD TRAPPING COUNTRIES

Trappers often want to get away from home and look for new trapping grounds in some distant section. Usually they inquire through the questions and answers department of some outdoor magazine about the trapping opportunities in some specific territory; then, if they receive a favorable reply, they procure and study maps of the region. Of course, such maps can only show the locations of streams, lakes, ponds, woods, and mountains; they do not give much definite information about the fur game to be found there, its plentifulness or scarcity. There is nothing particularly wrong with this idea, provided one visits the territory in question and personally prospects it before going to the expense of outfitting and perhaps wasting time in establishing a trap line there. Not infrequently, after one carefully examines the territory, one comes to the conclusion that better trapping may be had on one's home trapping grounds and calls off the whole thing.

There are certain parts of the country, however, that offer much better trapping than that which is found in others. Sometimes the general trapping may be rather poor in these sections, but the trapping for certain species of fur-bearers may be very good. Hence, Michigan, New York, New Jersey, Maryland, and Louisiana have considerable marsh land where good muskrat trapping may be found. However, some of this marsh land is commercialized, being controlled by owners who either hire expert trappers to trap their muskrats, or lease out certain marsh acreages to trappers on a percentage basis. The "outside" trapper in these sections may find most of the best areas posted. He may even be unable to find available suitable trapping territory. There is, however, good muskrat trapping to be had in the marshes and lowlands in almost every state in the United States, as well as in many regions in southern Canada. Oregon and Washington offer good muskrat trapping in certain sections, as do Missouri, Wisconsin, Kentucky, Indiana, Illinois, and Ohio.

Maine, New Hampshire, New York, Pennsylvania, and Michigan have good fox trapping. Ohio, Indiana, Illinois, Michigan, and Wisconsin are good states for the mink trapper, with Maine, New York, Oregon, and Washington being second choice. For skunks and raccoons, the regions drained by the Mississippi and Ohio rivers are very good. Coyotes and wolves are found mostly in the prairie lands and among the foothills in the Western countries. Timber wolves are found in the mountainous regions of western United States, as well as throughout many parts of Canada. Opossums are found most plentiful in the agricultural districts in central and southern United States.

For general trapping, Canada and the north half of the United States are good, principally because the terrain is suitable for fur game and the cooler temperatures in these sections produce better quality raw furs. For like reasons, Alaska is noted for its good trapping. More Southern regions frequently have an abundance of fur-bearing animals, but, because of the milder temperatures, they do not offer the profitable trapping that is often found in many sections of the country farther north.

Chapter III

Prospecting for Fur Game

Webster, in his dictionary, defines prospecting as the act of exploring or examining for something. And in prospecting for fur game, it is just that! We explore or examine an area for the tracks, signs, trails, and feeding grounds of the fur-bearing animals found there, which, if carefully done, will always give us sufficient information to enable us to trap the locality with some measure of success. If we always do this prospecting in a thorough and effective manner, we can set our traps with the assurance that they are likely to make catches; for we have made our sets at the most favorable of the places we have previously located and with full knowledge of the kinds of fur-bearers for which we are trapping. We know where these animals are using, where they are denning, what they

11

are feeding on, and something of their movements from day to day.

To a great extent, prospecting a locality often determines the true route of the trap line. One will sometimes find that fur game is apparently frequenting a certain area in plenty; this makes it advisable to change the general direction of the trap line in order to reach that locality. Or a group of dens, a willow-choked bayou, a tangle of trails, or a rocky cliff may offer trapping opportunities that justify changing the trap line to enable one to trap these places. The trap line, therefore, is a rather unstable thing; and prospecting is a big factor in shaping it.

Prospecting an area is a very important procedure, a vital part of the preparatory work of trapping. It is much like blueprinting in construction work, in that it gives one a sort of groundwork upon which to build. Armed with the knowledge gained by prospecting, a trapper can go to work with the feeling that he is going to meet with more than a modicum of success, even if he is operating in strange, new territory. He has not only become familiar with every little nook and corner of the area in which he expects to do his trapping, but he has also learned much about the habits and movements of the fur game found there.

Kinds of Fur Game

At first thought, it may seem somewhat redundant to enumerate the various kinds of animals that are of interest to trappers, since their names are known to nearly everyone. However, some readers may be beginning trappers who have not become familiar with any great number of the kinds of animals that have pelts with market value. Others may know about the fur-bearers found in their parts of the country, but would like to know more about some of the animals in other sections. So before going further into the details of prospecting, it has been thought advisable to give a list of the principal animals that are commonly trapped for their pelts, together with a few words of information about them. It should be remembered, however, that there are often many subspecies of some of these kinds of fur-bearing animals which vary quite a bit in color, size, and distribution.

Weasel—Smaller than the mink; found in practically all parts of the country; brown in the summer, white with black-tipped tails in the winter (in Northern sections) ; pelt, of some value; white-furred skins most valuable.

Ermine—Somewhat larger than the weasel; fur, white; tail black tipped; pelt, of considerable value.

Mink—Measures twelve to eighteen inches from the tip of the nose to the root of the tail; distributed throughout almost all parts of the country; fur, dark and glossy; pelt, valuable. Cotton mink, a sport or mutation, not a distinct species; brown guard hairs; whitish, coarse, cottonlike fur next to the skin; pelt, of little value.

Marten—Larger than the mink; found generally at high altitudes in mountainous country throughout western United States and in many parts of Canada; fur, dark to brown; pelt, very valuable.

Fisher—Measures twenty-four to twenty-six inches from the tip of the nose to the root of the tail; found throughout the northern parts of the country, and in Canada; pelt, valuable.

Red Fox—Measures from twenty to thirty inches from the tip of the nose to the root of the tail; found in practically all sections of the United States; fur, reddish brown; pelt, of good value. Gray Fox—Smaller than the red fox; found throughout nearly all Southern sections of the United States; fur, coarse; guard hairs, tipped with gray; pelt, not of great value.

There are several other species of foxes, including the Black Fox, the Kitt Fox, the Swift Fox, the White Fox, the Blue Fox, and the Silver Fox. Many of these are found only in the far Northern regions.

Timber Wolf—Measures from five to seven feet; inhabits the western parts of the United States and many parts of Canada; fur, grayish or dark gray; pelt, not highly valuable.

Coyote—Small wolf; inhabits the western parts of the United States and many sections in the southern part of Canada; fur, coarse, rufus, or grayish; pelt, not highly valuable.

Black Bear—This animal will often weigh from five hundred to six hundred pounds; found only in the wild places in the United States, and in some parts of Canada; fur, long, black, lustrous; pelt, valuable.

There are several species of bears in North America, including the Black Bear, the Grizzly Bear, the Brown Bear, the Cinnamon Bear, and the Polar Bear.

Raccoon—This animal measures from thirty to thirty-six inches in length, measuring from the tip of the nose to the tip of the tail. It is found practically throughout North America. Fur, reddish-brown in the Southern sections to a very dark color in the Northern sections; pelt, of fair value.

Skunk—Found in nearly all parts of the United States, as well as in parts of southern Canada. There are several species and sub-species of skunks. Skunk skins are classed as black, short striped, narrow striped, and broad striped, according to the amount of white appearing on them. Aside from the texture and glossiness of the fur, the value of a skunk skin lies principally in the amount of black fur on it. The more black there is in a skunk skin, the more valuable the skin is.

Opossum—Smaller than the raccoon; found in the eastern half of the United States, from New York to Florida; fur, wooly texture, creamy white; pelt, low in value.

Beaver—Measures thirty-four to thirty-eight inches from the tip of the nose to the root of the tail; found in scattered sections in northern and western United States, and in Canada; being re-stocked in places; fur, fine, silky; pelt, valuable.

Otter—Smaller than the beaver; found, rather rarely, throughout North America; fur, dark, silky, glossy; pelt, valuable.

Muskrat—Measures from twelve to sixteen inches from the tip of its nose to the root of its tail; found in nearly all parts of North America from the Gulf of Mexico northward; fur, soft, rich brown to black; pelt, fairly valuable.

Advantages of Early Prospecting

There are many advantages in prospecting the trapping grounds early. Prospecting should be done at least several weeks before the opening of the trapping season. Late summer is not too early for this work. Early autumn is better than at a later time, but not so good as the earlier period. Never should prospecting be put off until time for putting out the traps. Many inexperienced trappers do just this. In fact, some few overlook entirely the matter of prospecting the area to be covered in trapping; they just start out with a pack of traps, expecting to find places for good sets as they go along. It scarcely need be said that they are missing a lot of good trapping in practicing such slipshod methods of working. One never comes to know too much about conditions on one's trapping grounds; and in no other way can one come by such knowledge except by good prospecting.

Early prospecting not only enables one to become familiar with an area before going into it to set traps, but it gives one valuable information about the movements of the animals found therein sufficiently far in advance of the trapping season to enable one to make good use of it. Thus, one is better able to locate good places for sets, since one knows just where the animals are using and what they are feeding on. Too, one can look up dens, build bait cubbies, and map out a general route for his trap lines. Sometimes one may want to "bait up" certain favorable set locations by leaving bait where the animals will become accustomed to feeding on it. And, too, when prospecting has been done early, one will have more time for examining and repairing the various articles in one's trapping outfit, as well as for doing the many little jobs necessary in preparing for an active trapping season.

Observation, the Key to Good Prospecting

Good prospecting cannot be accomplished without close observation. Paying attention to the things one sees, such as tracks, signs, set locations, and the like, and judging their value and significance in relation to the coming trapping activities constitute much of the value of prospecting a trapping ground. Everyone does not have the ability to observe closely. Some few have it as an inherent aptitude; others acquire it by carefully training the power of attention; and a few, because of the lack of natural ability, never can hope to acquire it. Some have the ability to observe closely, yet cannot apply the knowledge thus gained to the art of trapping, to the business of setting traps for fur game. As a rule, though, almost any person who has this ability developed to a high degree makes a good trapper. Yet one who is a poor observer can often do much to improve his trapping by putting forth determined effort in studying—both in books and on the trapping ground—everything relating to trapping. After all, a deep interest in everything pertaining to trapping and a burning desire to become a successful trapper can take one a long way along the road to success.

Sometimes a mere claw-mark will lead the trapper to discover the denning-place of an animal. Or maybe a few hairs on a splintered rail at an opening where a trail passes beneath a rail fence will be the clue that leads to the capture of a fox, or perhaps to the capture of two or three foxes. Or possibly a few fragments of flag root at a drift in a stream may result in the catching of half a dozen muskrats. The apparently insignificant little things like these can often mean much to the trapper. So when prospecting keep your mind alert to the possibilities of all such apparently inconsequential signs—they may often be the means of making you far more successful in your trapping than you think. The expert trapper never lets anything escape his notice, no matter how unimportant or insignificant it may appear to be. That is why he is an expert. If you wish to catch more fur game, you should do likewise.

Use of Maps and Notebooks in Prospecting

Your first exploring trip in the new trapping ground should be of a sort of cursory nature—a rather quick excursion for the purpose of getting the "lay of the land" and ascertaining the kinds and approximate numbers of fur-bearing animals using in the area. Don't spend a lot of time now looking for set locations. That will come later. Carry a notebook and pencil and jot down what you find—the characteristics of the topography of the area (streams, hills, roads, woods, lakes, swamps) and the various places where tracks and signs show that there are plenty of fur-bearing animals using in the vicinity. Locate feeding grounds of any appreciable extent. Be accurate and specific. Indicate the exact location of anything mentioned, setting down size (if it is a lake, stream, etc.), areas (if it is woods, hills, feeding grounds, and the like), and approximate numbers (if the notes cover tracks, dens, evidence of the presence of animals, etc.). When you get home, draw a rather detailed map of the area, indicating thereon everything you have jotted down in your notebook. Use pen and ink and a heavy grade of good paper in this work, showing thereon the directions and scaling the map to indicate mileage.

You now have a set of rough notes pertaining to the area you expect to trap and a sort of skeletonized map of the grounds. These

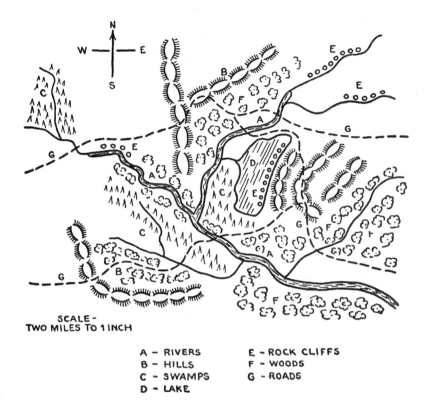

SCALE -
TWO MILES TO 1 INCH

A – RIVERS	E – ROCK CLIFFS
B – HILLS	F – WOODS
C – SWAMPS	G – ROADS
D – LAKE	

Skeletonized Map of Trapping Grounds. Detailed sectional maps incorporating notebook material should be made from this skeletonized map for use in the field.

will form a basis for your future prospecting here. Use your notebook for jotting down on-the-spot information on every trip you make to the area. You can readily transfer this information to the map upon your return home. You will now want to notice particularly any tracks, dens, signs, or set locations that you find. Set down in your notebook all information about these that will be helpful in future trapping. But remember to keep your notes fluid, so that changes can be made as circumstances dictate. This preliminary work will give you a sort of blueprint of the trapping grounds, a working plan that will be invaluable in the days to come, when you are actively engaged in trapping in the area.

V. J. C.

Chapter IV

About Equipment

Next to skill, nothing is quite so important in trapping as the selection of equipment. Beginning trappers seldom give sufficient thought to the choosing of the outfit, too often being satisfied with poor or defective traps, unsuitable fur stretchers, clothing unfit for outdoor use, and poor equipment of all kinds. Experienced trappers, however, usually select equipment with care. They know something of the hard use to which equipment is subjected, so they choose an outfit with this thought uppermost in mind. They look for quality in the articles they purchase, knowing that only items of sterling worth can possibly give satisfactory service in outdoor use.

The trapping outfit should always be chosen with an eye to lightness and compactness; yet it must be substantial and well able to take the hard knocks that it is most certain to get on difficult trips in rough terrain. Such an outfit may well consist of traps, fur stretchers, clothing, packsack, gun, boat or snowshoes, cooking utensils, articles for personal use, and the very few miscellaneous articles needed to carry on trapping activities in wilderness or semi-wilderness countries. Of course there will be food supplies, too. Such an outfit may be modified for use in trapping in farming communities or near settled districts, where additional purchases may be made at any time.

SELECT GOOD EQUIPMENT

In selecting trapping equipment, the thing of paramount importance is quality. Get good equipment, even if you have to pay what appears to be a big price. Poor equipment is too costly at any price. A cheap outfit will need renewal within a few years, at most; and, without doubt, the service it has given will have been anything but satisfactory. Poorly made traps will break or maybe be so defective that they will not catch and hold animals; inferior guns may jam or otherwise fail at an inopportune time; clothing of poor quality will wear out quickly, or at least will give unsatisfactory service; defective cooking utensils will not last well; and many other articles in the cheap outfit will be found to be either defective or of very poor quality, either of which can mean much trouble to a busy trapper, especially if he happens to be operating in wilderness country.

The outfit does not have to be an elaborate one. In fact, a simple trapping outfit consisting of the right articles is the one that will be most useful. If you find use for each and every article in the outfit and find nothing therein that could be eliminated without missing it greatly, then you have done well in choosing the items of equipment. "Travel light, but right" is a good thought to keep in mind when selecting the trapping outfit.

TRAPS AND FUR STRETCHERS

The modern steel trap, if it is of good make, is a smoothly operating, effective device for capturing wild animals. However, a poorly made steel trap, or one made of defective material, can be an abomination. Remember, one valuable fur-bearer lost by a poorly made or defective trap could well pay for several good traps.

When buying traps study trap types in order to know just what kind of traps you need. There are many types—long spring, underspring, double-jaw, two-trigger, and others. Each type has a particular use—underspring for lightness and compactness, to be used in narrow places; double-jaw for trapping those kinds of fur-bearers that are in the habit of twisting or gnawing out of the trap, etc. Set and spring the trap. Watch the trigger action, and the way the trap snaps shut when tripped. The pan should set level and be on a slightly higher plane than that of the jaws. See that it drops downward smoothly when the trap is sprung. Watch for weakness in the jaws or in the spring. Examine the trap chain for weakness. It should be well made, strong, and be provided with a swivel. Examine the trap throughout for flaws in material.

Here are some modern trap types, along with their outstanding features and distinctive operating peculiarities. Each has its particular uses. It would be well worth any trapper's time to study all these trap types carefully. Only a few of these will be discussed briefly.

Among all trap types, the long-spring Victor Stop-Loss trap is perhaps as good as any. Very popular among muskrat trappers, it is not too heavy, is easy to set, and the delayed-action third guard jaw largely prevents wring-offs and escapes. While this trap is a little more expensive than the standard trap, its effectiveness and holding power make it well worth the extra cost. This same stop-loss feature is built into a special Oneida Jump trap, which, because of the compactness and lightness of the trap, makes it even more desirable for some uses than the long-spring trap.

Another type of trap worth mentioning is the Oneida Victor Coil-Spring trap. Made in several sizes, its lightning-fast action, compactness, and strength, together with its light weight, make it unexcelled for use in trapping such animals as the mink, the marten, the skunk, the raccoon, and the weasel and muskrat. This trap lies very flat when set, making it very easy to cover. The heavier trap with its jaw spread of 5⅝" is a splendid fox trap, while the smaller traps are undoubtedly the best mink traps on the market.

The Blake and Lamb Double Underspring trap is so durable, so sturdy in construction, and so fast in action that special mention here is a must. It has no peer as a fox trap. The Sure-Hold Long-Spring type is just about as escape-proof as a trap can be. The Hawkins Company also makes an Underspring Sure-Hold trap which is very sturdy, compact, and certain in action. It makes the use of drowning devices and light drags unnecessary. This company also makes a Long-Spring Double-Jaw trap that is very effective in preventing captured animals from escaping by gnawing off a foot.

The Victor Conibear is a body-gripping wire trap of deadly performance. Lightweight, compact, and easily set on land or in snow or water, it is the first practical humane killer trap ever made. Different sizes are available. Being constructed of strong steel wire and activated by a powerful coil spring. it is both durable and effective. In fact, it is one of the surest traps on the market. There are other killer traps, but none quite so good as the Victor Conibear.

There is a class of traps on the market that is designed to capture animals alive and unhurt. One might say, in fact, that these traps are merely improved box traps, since their structural parts and operating designs are practically the same as those of the old-fashioned traps that were so attractive to boy trappers in the past. They are good traps, however, and can be relied on to do a fine job of capturing game. Excellent for trapping animals for stocking purposes or for taking animals unhurt, they serve their purpose very well. The Haveaheart Company at Ossining, New York, and the Johnson Company at Waverly, Kentucky, make two of the more outstanding traps of this type.

Trappers may procure their traps from various sources. One of the best places to purchase traps is at S. Stanley Hawbaker and Sons, Fort Loudon, Pennsylvania. Other good reliable sources are Sears Roebuck and Company, Chicago, Illinois; Montgomery Ward, Chicago, Illinois; Daileys Trapper Supply House, Odgensburg, N.Y.; your local hardware dealer. Information concerning various makes of traps and sources of supply may be had by writing The Hawkins Company, America's Oldest Trap Manufacturers, South Britain, Conn., or Animal Trap Company of America, Lititz, Pennsylvania.

There is wide variation in the preference for traps among the trappers. Some like the Victor traps. They are good in the low-priced field. The Blake and Lamb traps are good ones. Without a doubt, the Oneida Newhouse traps are best. Manufactured since 1848, they are without a peer. They cost slightly more than some other traps, but they are strong, durable, smooth and certain in action. Snares may be purchased of Raymond Thompson, Alderwood Manor, Washington; or they may be had from almost any dealer in trappers' supplies.

There are two things every trapper should have as part of his equipment: extension trap chains and large "S" links. The extension chains come in various sizes. They can be used for increasing the length of standard trap chains, for repairing broken links or damaged parts of chains, and for other repairs that keep coming up in the trapper's equipment. The "S" links are handy for fastening extra chains to traps, for fastening pronged drags or grapples to traps, and for fastening two traps together to prevent wring-offs. Other uses will be found.

Steel traps are made in various sizes. Here are the right sizes for use in trapping the various fur-bearing animals. These sizes are for use when trapping with the long spring trap.

No. 0—Weasel, gopher. No. 1—Muskrat, weasel, mink, skunk, opossum. No. 1½—Mink, skunk, opossum, raccoon, fox. No. 2—Fox, lynx, raccoon. No. 3—Otter, fox. No. 4—Beaver, coyote, wolf. No. 5—Bear. No. 6—Grizzly bear.

It will be noticed that in a few of the listings given here two different sized traps are recommended for trapping one kind of animal. This is because the opinions of trappers in various sections differ in regard to the best size for use in trapping for these animals.

Traps are of several kinds and styles. For instance, we have the No. 1 long-spring style Victor trap. Then we have the Sure-Hold traps, the Double-Jaw traps, the Coil-Spring traps, even specially made wire traps. Frequently some of these various styles are numbered differently to the standard traps. No. 1 (standard trap) and "corresponding size" means these other various styles of traps are of the same size as the No. 1 standard trap. In the Oneida Newhouse traps, we have the No. 4 with spread of jaws of 6½"; the No. 14 with spread of jaws of 6½"; the No. 48 with spread of jaws of 6½"—all different types of traps. The Blake and Lamb famous No. 21 trap with spread of jaws of 5½" "corresponds" with the No. 1½ Oneida Jump trap with spread of jaws of 5⅛"—or practically so.

The number of traps you will need depends on the kind of trapping you want to do and the locality in which the trapping is to be done. If you are trapping by boat along a lake shore or stream, your supply of traps need not be limited; but if you are packing in to a trapping ground on foot, remember to keep the total weight of your pack down to fifty or seventy pounds, depending on your size and build. Of course, when more than one pack trip in is to be made, then you can have more traps in the outfit. Usually six to eight dozen traps of various sizes will be needed, especially if the trap line is to be in wilderness territory. Perhaps half this number would be sufficient for trapping in farming communities.

Fur stretchers are another headache when it comes to transporting them in on foot to a trapping ground. Some trappers use the light wire stretchers, which reduces weight and bulk, and makes transporting easier. Wire stretchers can be made in camp, shaped and put together, using No. 9 wire and a base block of soft wood. Other trappers, however, prefer the board stretchers, and they struggle along somehow with them. When trapping by boat, or when trapping in farming communities where there are no long packs to be made, the problem of transportation is, of course, greatly simplified. Backwoods trappers frequently use flexible sprouts for making fur stretchers. They can be made in camp, after the trapper has become located on his trapping ground. Of course these stretchers are more or less makeshifts, and are not always satisfactory.

The board stretcher is made of soft pine, poplar, or other soft wood. It is about half an inch thick, some twenty-three to thirty-three inches or more in length (depending on the length of the skin to be stretched), and some four to eight inches in width. It is shaped to the general form of the skin to be stretched, tapered slightly, and thinned out toward the edges, leaving the central part the original thickness. The edges are then rounded slightly.

Some trappers like the wedge stretcher, which is an improvement on the one just mentioned. However, it is more trouble to make. It is made identical with the one just described, except that it is a trifle wider to allow for a wedge piece being sawed from its middle. This wedge piece is one inch wide at its wide end (which is at the wide end of the stretcher), and three eighths of an inch wide at the other end of the stretcher. All sawed edges are sandpapered down to a smooth, slick finish. In using this wedge piece, insert the two halves of the board in the skin, introduce the wedge piece between them, then drive in this piece until the skin is properly stretched. A few tacks along the edges of the skin keep the pelt in shape while it is curing. This fur stretcher is sometimes called the three-piece stretcher.

Fur stretchers of these types are used only for stretching "cased" skins. "Open" skins are usually stretched on wide, flat boards, in frames, or on hoops made of flexible withes.

Here are some stretcher sizes:

	Length	Width at the base	Width at the shoulder
Mink:	36 in.	4 in.	3 in.
Muskrat:	24 in.	8 in.	7 in.
Raccoon:	42 in.	12 in.	10 in.
Fox:	48 in.	10 in.	6½ in.
Weasel:	16 in.	3 in.	2 in.
Skunk:	34 in.	10 in.	7½ in.
Marten:	34 in.	4 in.	3 in.
Fisher:	45 in.	9 in.	8 in.
Otter:	48 in.	8 in.	7 in.

CLOTHING, PACKS, AND GUNS

Trappers need to dress for warmth, especially when working in Northern sections. Blankets and sleeping bags are often rabbit-skin lined to make them warmer. A good clothing outfit for use in northern sections may well consist of woolen underclothes, heavy woolen outer shirt, mackinaw, cloth trousers (with lace-up legs) and jacket, and two pairs of heavy woolen socks. Extra clothing will, of course, be needed for making changes. The pac makes excellent footwear for the northern countries; but get those with leather uppers and rubber bottoms. Soft pacs, however, will be needed for snowshoe wear.

For trapping in sections farther south, lighter clothing may be used—light wool or standard hunting clothing, or even the lighter khaki clothing in the extreme Southern territories. Rubber boots will be needed for swamp and stream trapping. The trapper's clothing commonly undergoes severe wear. To last well, it must be good.

Blankets, of course, are a necessity, whether one uses an established home camp or traps on a long line with several overnight camps. Get good, heavy, woolen blankets, and be sure you have plenty to keep you warm. Sleeping bags are a boon to trappers. But get a good one. Poor ones are an abomination.

Most wilderness or semiwilderness trappers find the packsack or pack basket unexcelled for getting the supplies in to the home camp. Whether your choice is the packsack or the pack basket, be sure it has wide, heavy leather or web shoulder straps. Narrow, flimsy shoulder straps can be pretty much of an aggravation on a long carry when they become rolled or twisted. A tump line fitted to go on the fore part of the head will help wonderfully in resting the shoulders occasionally on long trips.

Some trappers like the haversack for carrying traps. It can be made roomy, and is not much in the way in getting around among the bushes and rocks. It is usually carried by a heavy strap over the shoulder, and is handy when removing traps for making sets. It can be made out of heavy waterproof canvas or other strong, heavy material.

The trapper usually will not have much use for a gun, other than for killing bait for traps, since he will not often have much time for hunting. For this purpose, a light pistol of small caliber will be needed. A single-shot will do; but a good magazine gun is often handier. The automatic pistol is very good. It should be a 22 cal., using long-rifle cartridges.

A good rifle sometimes comes in handy when trapping in wilderness countries. It can be of service in laying in the winter supply of meat in good deer territory. Although there are many models of big-game rifles, the average trapper in heavy woods country will often find the 30-30 carbine about suits his needs.

OTHER EQUIPMENT

It may be well to mention a few other necessary items of equipment. These need not be many. Most of them are personal items, and should be duplicated for each person when two or more go on the trip.

A good, heavy pocketknife is indispensable. It can be used for skinning game, cutting trap stakes, making drowning poles, or may even be found useful for kitchen work. No other knife will be needed. Some carry a sheath knife; but I never have found one very useful on the trap line. However, a good, light belt axe or trapping hatchet is a very handy tool on the trap line, as well as in camp, for many jobs that are beyond the capacity of the pocketknife.

Anyone going into wilderness or semi-wilderness territory to trap should have a good axe. It is an indispensable tool in a backwoods camp. A camp light is needed, too. This may be a carbide lamp, a gasoline or kerosene lantern, or candles. Gasoline or kerosene is difficult to transport, especially on back-pack trips. For this reason, the carbide lamp or the candle is preferable. Snowshoes and toboggans are needed when trapping in far northern countries. Don't forget to take a sewing kit, ditty bag of toilet articles, waterproof match container, compass (if going into a strange, wild section), medicine kit, and a "life-saver" kit. The latter should contain a rigged fishing line, hooks, staging, friction tape, waterproofed matches, fire kindlers made of old photographic negatives film or paraffined paper, a few raisins, and a little chocolate candy.

Useless Equipment

A few words about useless equipment may not be amiss. Beginning trappers, and even some who are more experienced and should know better, often take with them into the woods a lot of useless equipment. Don't take more traps than you will use. Don't take a lot of superfluous clothing or provisions. Estimate your needs carefully, and live up to that estimate. Don't take a lot of fishing and hunting gear, if you are going to trap, as you probably won't have much time to hunt or fish. As a rule, one should not take musical instruments, library books, or other recreational equipment. When two trappers work together, a pack of playing cards or a set of dominos may come in handy when storm-bound. A good, light camera can often be used to advantage.

Reliable trappers' supplies may be had from Daileys Trapper Supply House, Odgensburg, N.Y.; S. Stanley Hawbaker and Sons, Fort Loudon, Penn.; Sears Roebuck and Company, Chicago, Illinois; or Montgomery Ward, Chicago, Illinois. Many of the bigger fur companies carry a line of traps and trappers' supplies.

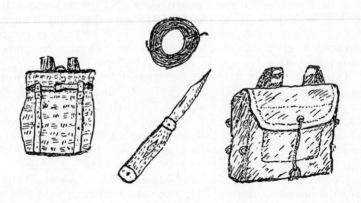

Chapter V

Modern Trapping Methods

Just as farming and mining have undergone many changes throughout the years, so has trapping been modernized to meet the needs of changing conditions. Thus, deadfall trapping and snaring have largely given way to the use of the more modern steel trap. And even the steel trap has been improved in many ways, such as by equipping it with double jaws, triple-clutch jaws, extra jaw and trigger, and the like. The underspring and coil-spring type of traps have come into use, as well as various models of wire traps and others. Too, trappers nowadays less often tend long lines of traps with the use of overnight camps, since most trapping is done in farming communities; and this fact, of course, has to some extent affected outfitting. While skill in trapping is as much needed today as it ever has been—possibly more needed than in the early days— the methods of employing traps for catching fur game have some-what changed, as well as the ways of tending a trap line and caring for the raw furs.

Old-time trappers either put out long lines of traps in wilderness regions, tending them on foot, or trapped from a boat, or, in the prairie countries, they frequently trapped on horseback. But nowadays we find trappers establishing auto trap lines of many miles in extent, setting their traps in spots where the signs and tracks of animals lead them to believe there is good trapping. Boat trapping is still widely practiced on streams and lakes; trapping on horseback is still in vogue in certain sections in the West; but the long-line trappers have given way largely to trappers who use shorter lines in more restricted territories, except, perhaps, in a few places in the mountainous regions in western United States and throughout much of the wilder parts of Canada. "Spot trapping," which is the trapping of only the choice spots or "fur pockets" in a wide territory, is a frequent practice of trappers nowadays. This method of trapping is particularly suited for use on auto trap lines, where much territory can be covered each day.

Various Methods of Trapping

Trappers now use many methods of trapping that were unknown to the old-time trapper. Most trapping in early days was done by using baited or unbaited deadfalls and snares. The only steel traps in those days were blacksmith-made, and were mostly costly, crude affairs. Few were in use. Therefore blind sets were unknown; and few trail sets or den sets were used. Now and then an enterprising trapper would deviate from bait trapping to set a few snares or deadfalls in trails; but no doubt most fur-bearers were caught in baited traps.

The trapper of today knows that he must use many different methods of setting traps. Only in this way can he make the most of his trapping opportunities. He therefore chooses the type of set best suited to the surroundings, keeping in mind the fact that weather conditions and variations in animal habits may cause him to change to a different type of set at any time. He makes use of sets of all kinds—trail sets, blind sets, den sets, bait sets, and any other type of set that will enable him to outwit the animal he is trying to capture. Both natural and artificial lures and scents of many kinds are frequently used, for trapping nowadays is largely a matter of pitting one's trapping knowledge against the cunning and sagacity of the wild animals. Anything, therefore, that will enable one to make sets that will not arouse the suspicions of an animal is the thing to strive for.

"Spot Trapping"

Trappers nowadays often find it to their advantage sort of to bunch their traps. They often work over a wide area, placing traps only in the best trapping spots they can find. Such trapping is known as "spot trapping," since the trapper sets his traps only at spots where lots of signs and tracks are found. Only the best spots of a given area are trapped, thus eliminating the poorer places and those parts where few signs of fur game may be found.

"Spot trapping" is often very profitable. It has several advantages over other kinds of trapping. When one "fur pocket" is trapped out, another near by or at some distance away can usually be located and trapped with profit. The use of an automobile or in some cases a boat, makes spot trapping possible, since it shortens distances between the "fur pockets" and enables one to cover much territory in a short time.

Auto Trap Lines

Trapping by automobile has become rather popular in recent years, especially in those sections where good roads are plentiful. It has many advantages over trapping on foot. It eliminates the problem of carrying traps; it enables one to cover a lot of territory; it saves much time in getting about from one good trapping spot to another; it enables one to carry all needed equipment; and it increases one's chances for trapping success, since it enables one to do all one's trapping in the best places. Too, the auto trap line enables one to do long-line trapping without bothering about overnight camps. However, it is sometimes a difficult matter to reach the better trapping places by automobile on account of bad roads. Then one is often forced to do much foot work. But it is surprising the way some trappers get around over rugged country with the automobile.

When planning to trap a territory by automobile, it is a good idea to carry duplicate parts for the machine, such as spark plugs, points, light bulbs, brake kits, etc. Especially is this true if one plans to trap in wilderness or semiwilderness territories. A supply of gasoline and oil will be needed for long stays. And permanent anti-freeze for the radiator is a must. Be sure it is of such strength that it will safely withstand any low temperatures that may come. And carry a small supply for replacement in case of accidental loss. As for the machine itself, see that it is a good one—mechanically.

Don't, under any circumstances, attempt to use an old worn-out automobile on the trap line. Such a car will be only an aggravation; and most trappers have enough of this commodity from their everyday work without inviting an extra supply from such a car.

TRAPPING BY BOAT

Most of the old-time trappers who did much trapping along lake shores or streams early learned the value of trapping by boat. They found they could set their traps to better advantage by using a boat. The sets were easier made; they were easier located from the water; and they proved to be better game-takers than those that were made from the shore. Then, too, these trappers soon saw that they could get around better in a boat; and not only that, but they could carry more traps and equipment with them. Modern trap-

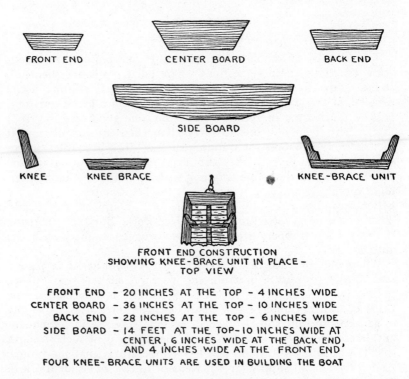

FRONT END

CENTER BOARD

BACK END

SIDE BOARD

KNEE   KNEE BRACE   KNEE-BRACE UNIT

FRONT END CONSTRUCTION
SHOWING KNEE-BRACE UNIT IN PLACE -
TOP VIEW

FRONT END – 20 INCHES AT THE TOP – 4 INCHES WIDE
CENTER BOARD – 36 INCHES AT THE TOP – 10 INCHES WIDE
BACK END – 28 INCHES AT THE TOP – 6 INCHES WIDE
SIDE BOARD – 14 FEET AT THE TOP – 10 INCHES WIDE AT
CENTER, 6 INCHES WIDE AT THE BACK END,
AND 4 INCHES WIDE AT THE FRONT END
FOUR KNEE-BRACE UNITS ARE USED IN BUILDING THE BOAT

A Good Trapping Boat.

pers, too, were quick to see these advantages. So most trappers today use a boat in stream or lake trapping.

The trapper's boat should be strong and fairly light, not too long, say, about fourteen to sixteen feet, thirty-eight inches wide at the center and thirty-four inches at the back end, with gunwales around ten inches in width. The front end should be a little wider than that of most boats, since the trapper may often want to work at this end when making sets. It should be constructed of white pine or cedar. Equip the boat with oars for use in strong winds or where there is much current; but carry a paddle to use when creeping along near shore, or when moving about coves or bayous, or nosing around bush-grown points.

Trapping On Horseback

A big advantage of trapping on horseback is the ease with which heavy traps may be transported and the speed with which long distances may be covered. Then, too, horseback trappers nowadays can trap canyons, rocky sections, and bushy arroyos, where trappers on foot would find it next to impossible to get out their traps, and where the automobile trapper would simply be out of luck.

Long-Line Trapping On Foot

This kind of trapping is usually done in mountainous sections, and in heavily forested areas in wilderness or semiwilderness countries. Usually in this sort of trapping the main camp is centrally located in relation to the trapping grounds, with looped trap lines radiating in all directions, on which are established one or more overnight camps. Sometimes the trap lines are laid out in one elongated loop, with the main camp situated at a favorable location somewhere on that loop and overnight camps spaced along the course at points about a day's travel apart. No matter in what manner the trap lines are laid out, the main idea in long-line trapping is to get overnight camps so spaced that the trapper will be enabled to trap over a wide area, using his main camp as a storage place for supplies and fur skins.

This sort of trapping usually calls for plenty of hard work and no little fortitude. Often there are dangers to be encountered; and not infrequently hazardous struggle with stormy weather and lonesome travel in trackless wilderness are anything but inviting. Usually two trappers work together, sharing the shelter of the main camp and each operating on different loops of trap line. Good roomy packsacks are needed in such trapping, since not only a lot of provisions and supplies must be transported in to the main camp before trapping begins, but a great number of traps will have to be distributed out along the various trap lines. Too, much daily use of the packsack or haversack will be needed on the trail. Long-line trappers will want to carry a belt gun for killing small animals for bait; and a light belt axe or trapping hatchet will be most useful.

TRAPPING ANIMALS FOR BOUNTY

In some parts of the country, bounties are paid on certain predatory animals, such as the coyote, wolf, fox, and bobcat. Sometimes trappers in such sections do summer trapping for these animals. However, when such trapping is done, trappers should use every precaution to avoid catching those animals on which no bounty is paid. Otherwise, the damage done to such fur-bearers might well offset any money the trapper might make by bounty trapping.

There are certain types of sets that may be used in bounty trapping which are not likely to take unwanted fur-bearers. Such sets should be used whenever possible. Baits and lures cannot always be depended upon, since either will often attract several kinds of animals. One should therefore devise sets that will take only the animals one wants to trap.

One such set for coyotes, wolves, and foxes may be made by making a shallow bait hole in a conspicuous place and burying therein a few fox or wolf droppings. No other bait is necessary.

Urine Set for Foxes, Coyotes, and Wolves. Fox, coyote, or wolf urine is sprinkled about the bases of the bushes at the sets. Skeleton is used as bait.

Wolves, foxes, or coyotes will attempt to dig out the droppings and thus get in the trap set in the freshly excavated dirt at the mouth of the hole. A variation of this set may be made by using fresh bait and lure at the bait hole, then setting traps near by at the bases of small bushes, stumps, projecting points of rock, weathered stakes stuck aslant in the ground, using fox or wolf urine as a lure. The bait will attract animals to the vicinity of the hole, and before leaving they will investigate the urine sets and get in the traps. Only the wanted animals will be taken in such sets, since other animals will not be attracted to these urine sets.

Another set that is good to use when trapping for bounty is what is known as the "scratching-place" set. It is made by setting a trap on a sandy knoll or mound, covering it lightly with sand—which should be placed on paper or leaves—then making imitation claw-marks over and around the set with a sharp-pointed instrument or pointed stick. Usually a few drops of fox or wolf urine are sprinkled over or around the set. Such a set will take almost any animal of the canine family, but is seldom visited by other animals.

Trappers who trap bobcats for bounty often make use of hollow logs, trees, crevices in rocks, rock ledges, and the like for set locations. Some of these trappers use oil of catnip as a lure at these sets; others depend on the flesh of house-cats or bobcats for baits, as such baits seldom attract other animals. A very good set for bobcats can be made by placing a trap on an old log, concealing it well, and dropping a bait several feet away at the base of a stump or tree, where it may be easily seen by a passing animal. Bobcats not infrequently circle such baits before going in to them, and in doing so will invariably walk on the log on which the trap is set.

Chapter VI

Trapping Devices

Here are a few aides to better trapping that will be found to be dependable, quite easily put to use, and of no little worth. Use them at every opportunity.

DROWNING DEVICES

When trapping along lakes, ponds, or streams, one will do well to make use of some device to prevent the captured animal from escaping by twisting off or gnawing off a foot or leg. Usually, however, most water animals escape by twisting off a foot. Muskrat and mink are pretty good at this sort of thing. They will often twist off a foot within two or three hours after they get into the trap, especially when there are broken bones. It is natural for such animals to want to go to deep water as soon as they feel the restraining power of the trap. In their struggles to get away, they will twist the trap chain around a stake fastening, and keep on twisting until the foot is freed and left in the trap. For this reason, it is well to use a drowning pole or drowning wire when trapping for such animals.

The drowning pole is a very simple arrangement. It is a pole about eight or ten feet long and of such size as to permit the ring

34

of the trap chain to slide freely its entire length when placed thereon. See that there are no knots on it to prevent the ring from sliding freely; and select a pole with a fork near the larger end, so as to prevent the trap from sliding off. After the set has been made, slip the ring of the trap chain over the small end of the pole,

Drowning Wire and Drowning Pole—In Use—Traps in Place.

securing this end to the bank by means of a forked stick. The large, forked end of the pole should reach out into deep water. This arrangement works well in still waters, but will often be washed away in flood waters.

A more stable arrangement for drowning the catch, and one just as effective, may be made by using a wire anchored in deep water and fastened securely to a hidden stake on the bank. Such a drowning device can be used in connection with most any type of set, and will work well in streams with considerable current, as well as in still waters. It will withstand high waters fairly well, too. Rocks or pieces of iron or concrete make good anchors for such devices. The wire need not be too long—say, eight or ten feet, or of such length as to reach deep water.

The Drag or Clog

Inexperienced trappers often find their traps sprung and holding the foot of some animal. A good way to stop this loss is by making use of the drag or clog. Professional trappers use such contrivances regularly. In fact, when making sets for land animals, they seldom use any other method of fastening traps.

How Not to Fasten a Trap.

The drag or clog usually is a brush, stick, or other object that may be picked up near the set. It should be about the same weight as that of the animal for which one is trapping. A small branch or a pronged stick makes an excellent clog or drag, since such an object will appear natural in almost any surrounding and will easily become tangled among rocks or bushes to impede the progress of any animal that may be moving away with the trap. Select those that are found in the vicinity of the set, so that they will not appear too much out of place. It is a good plan to make the drag or clog appear still more natural by sprinkling a few dead leaves over it, or by throwing a small brush or two or three sticks across it. Do not, however, use this method of fastening traps when sets are made near water, because under such circumstances much loss can occur by animals getting into the water and swimming away with the drag or clog.

Not a few of the old-time trappers used the spring pole fastening, which consisted of a small sapling bent over and fastened to the trap by a sort of trigger arrangement such as to release the pole and allow it to spring upward when a catch was made. The idea back of this arrangement was not only to prevent the captured animal from gnawing off a foot or twisting out of the trap, but to get the catch up off the ground and out of the reach of prowling predatory animals. The disadvantage of such a contrivance is that the sapling often springs upward with such force that the trap is sometimes jerked off an animal's leg. This arrangement is seldom used any more.

Trap Placers

In recent years, several types of trap placers have appeared on the market. Such gadgets enable the trapper to place traps beneath cold water without wetting the hands or the gloves. Too, they are handy about setting traps back in rock crevices or other inaccessible places. Most types resemble a pair of crooked tongs, with a convenient hand grip or shield at the end of the handles. They are usually light, but substantially well made. The use of such a gadget will save one many cold fingers. Often they enable one to set traps in places where one otherwise might find it difficult or impossible to make a set. A good one will be found to be very useful on the trap line.

Trap Setting Tools

Trap setting tools are quite convenient for those trappers who use large traps. There are types for all kinds of traps; some will handle more than one type of trap. Since they enable the trapper to open and set heavy traps without the danger of getting the fingers pinched or maimed, they will be found most useful when trapping such animals as fox, otter, beaver, fisher, or bear.

Trap spring clamps are also useful when setting large traps. These come in several styles, and may be purchased. However, good common C-clamps may be used for holding the springs of large traps, but are less convenient and reliable. There are trap setters for long spring traps, underspring traps, and others. Choose those you need with an eye to compactness, lightness, and strength. But if you set many big traps, a good trap setter will save you a lot of trouble. It will quickly pay for itself in time and temper saved, to say nothing about the pinched fingers and, maybe, maimed hands.

Chapter VII

Trapping Tricks and Aids

Every trapper has certain little tricks and aids he uses to enable
him to make more catches. As a rule, the more of these he has, the
more successful will be his trapping. He comes by these in many
ways, but usually acquires them from his trapping experiences
throughout the years; although many of them may be learned from
trapping books, or from conversation with trappers. Some trappers
are rather disposed to keep secret their special knowledge and one
is not always so fortunate as to learn such tricks and aids from them.
Then the books and trapping magazines are his best bet, plus his
own observation.

But if the trapper will at all times keep his mind alert to the trapping possibilities when he is out on his trap lines, he will soon find himself in possession of many little knacks or peculiarities in his way of doing things that will prove to be of great worth in his future trapping.

NARROWING DOWN TRAILS

A very common trick of experienced trappers, and, strangely enough, one seldom thought of by the beginning trapper, is that of narrowing down the trail at the point where the trap is set in order to lead a passing animal to place a foot on the trap pan. This may be done by placing brush, chunks of wood, pieces of bark, or small stones at either side of the trail, narrowing down the traveled area to the approximate width of the trap. However, always see that whatever material is used fits in well with the surroundings and does not cause any unnaturalness in the looks of things at the set.

Trail Narrowed by Natural Obstructions.

Not infrequently one can use a small bush to narrow the trail, thrusting it upright into the ground, where it may be used as a clog fastening for the trap. Too, one often finds places where trails are narrowed by natural obstructions, such as stones, trees, logs, exposed roots, and the like. Such places make excellent locations for sets.

PLACING TRAPS

When setting out traps, the alert trapper will be quick to notice such set locations as openings in drifts, fences, floodgates, at culverts, and around log heaps and brush piles. Runways under overhanging banks, holes in haystacks and strawstacks, gullies and paths in old unused pastures, springs and narrow streams, runways in swamps and along bodies of water, and worn paths in thickets, all such places will be given close examination with the view of determining whether they are being used by fur game. Animals frequent such places when wandering about at night in search of food, quite often visiting them night after night. Make sure that all such places that show fresh signs of fur game are utilized in making sets.

When placing traps of the long-spring type in trails or runways, or when using them at nearly all of the various kinds of sets, always see that the spring is turned at an angle of some forty-five degrees from its natural position toward that jaw of the trap that is held rigid by the dog. When the trap is set in this manner, an animal will step into it without in any way disturbing it by clambering over a protruding spring. In narrow places or when it is necessary to place a trap in confined quarters, it is often better to use the underspring type of trap. Always set a trap with its bed plate in line with the direction of travel likely to be taken by an approaching animal.

Traps set at the openings to dens or in runways or trails should always be placed a little to one side of the central line, since here is where an animal is most likely to place its feet. The trap should be only a very little to one side of center, however, else it may be entirely outside the line of travel. This is a good trick to use, particularly when making den sets, because animals will invariably spread their feet slightly when entering or leaving a den.

Never, under any circumstances, set a trap on the surface of the ground. Always scoop out a shallow depression for it, lining it with moss, powdered rotten wood, crushed dead leaves, or the like. Set this way, the trap will have the pan on a level with the surface of the ground, which always enhances the chances for making a catch. Too, such a set will not only cover easier and better, but will also lessen the danger of the trap freezing in during cold weather. Should it become necessary to fasten the trap to a stake, root, post, or other fixture, always use a fairly long wire or a short extension chain. This allows the captured animal to move about with the trap.

Use of "Guide Sticks"

Animals will often follow worn trails as they prowl about in the woods and fields. This is a natural trait of all animals. Because of this, trails offer the trapper excellent set locations. But to make trail sets most effective, two things are needed—narrowing down the trail at the point where the trap is to be placed, and the use of some method of causing a passing animal to place a foot on the trap pan. This may be accomplished by making use of what, for want of a better name, may be called "guide sticks."

"Guide Sticks" in Use. Note Small Guide Stones.

These guide sticks are the finishing touch to the set. The set is made in the usual way, being careful to see that the trap is well covered and fastened to a light movable brush drag or clog. Then, when all is finished, place a stick the size of one's thumb, and some twelve or eighteen inches long, across the trail some two or three inches from the trap, the exact distance depending on the kind of animal one is expecting to pass that way. When an animal approaches such a set, it will invariably step over the stick rather than upon it. If the stick has been placed the right distance from the trap, it will cause the animal to place a foot on the trap pan.

When there are different sized animals using a trail, it is a good plan to use two guide sticks to each set, placing one near the trap and the other at a farther distance on the opposite side of the set. However, be sure to keep both guide sticks within reasonable distance of the trap, judging the position of each by estimating the span of the step of the animal for which it is used.

PREPARING TRAPS FOR SETTING

Almost all steel traps are very similar in operation, as far as the tripping arrangements are concerned. Trap pans move up and down freely and are held in position by a dog which, in turn, is kept in place by pressure of the trap spring on the jaws of the trap. It is most important to see that the parts of this mechanism are well adjusted, so that when the trap is set the pan will be held exactly horizontal, just slightly above the level of the jaws. Then the smooth downward movement of the pan—if only a small fraction of an inch—will be sufficient to release the dog, thereby tripping the trap instantly. This nice adjustment is accomplished by buckling the dog slightly, or by bending the dog lug inward or outward to shorten or lengthen the distance between it and the notch in the shank of the trap pan. Neat adjustment here is necessary to the smooth action of most traps, since few traps receive such adjustment at the factory.

Sectional Views of the Trigger Arrangement of a Trap, Showing Wrong and Proper Arrangement.

Traps are frequently boiled with walnut bark or green walnut hulls before they are to be set, in order to discolor them and remove any human scent they may have about them. Logwood chips are not infrequently used for this purpose; and they are good. Some trappers prefer dipping their traps in a solution of melted beeswax or tallow. Whichever method is used, care should be taken to do the job in a thorough manner, seeing that all parts of the traps are covered well by the solution. Many trappers first oil their traps, then hang them in the smoke of burning feathers or burning green branches of pine or cedar. Such treatment is supposed to remove all human scent and put the traps in the best condition for setting. However, never touch the traps with bare hands after this work has been done. Hang them up, handling them only with gloved hands. It is best to use only clean leather or rubberized gloves for handling traps.

POINTERS ON SUCCESSFUL TRAPPING

The two great essentials of successful trapping are to locate the haunts and feeding grounds of fur game, then set traps where the animals are using, concealing the sets so well that creatures of the wild will never detect any change in the surroundings. Failure in trapping is often due to too much tracking about sets by trappers, or to the unnatural use of baits or scents. Not infrequently failure to conceal the trap and set so as to conform with the surroundings has much to do with the "poor luck" of the trapper. When making a set, we must always remember that our main object is to outwit wild animals, which are always unduly suspicious of any strange scent, or of even the slightest change in familiar surroundings. For these reasons, it is poor policy to spit or drop cigarette stubs or tobacco crumbs about a set, just as it is to do too much tracking about, or to leave fresh dirt, bits of paper, or freshly broken twigs or sticks lying about. To succeed in trapping, a man has to be just a little smarter than the animals he expects to catch.

Here are a few pointers that trappers will do well to keep in mind. Many of these have been learned the hard way—by trial and error, often after much wearisome trap-line work.

When a catch is made, kill the animal without unduly disturbing the surroundings, then reset and carefully cover the trap exactly as is was before, being sure to rearrange things as near as possible like they were before the catch had been made. Even if some disturbance shows in the vicinity of the set, don't let that fact bother you too much. The chances are good for making another catch here if you will manage things well, since some kinds of animals are prone to investigate any place that shows signs of having been visited by another animal.

When in doubt about animals frequenting a certain spot, place small pieces of bait at strategic points in that vicinity. If upon visiting the place next morning, one finds the baits gone, one may take it as a good indication that an animal has been prowling about the spot.

A killing set for opossums, skunks, raccoons, and foxes may be made by setting a trap alongside a half-rotten log beneath thick bushes on or near a stream bank and scattering thereabouts a handful of bird feathers. Or by setting a well-hidden trap at the base of a fruiting persimmon tree.

One of the surest sets I have ever used is made by placing a trap on a log that spans a stream. When traveling about the woods, animals find such logs and use them regularly as crossing places. Chop a notch—or if the log is partly rotten gouge out a depression—deep enough so that when the trap is set therein the jaws will be level with the surface of the log. Cover the trap with powdered rotten wood or dry moss; and, if possible, fasten it by using a light drag or a long piece of tough wire. The set should be made near one end of the log rather than near the middle. This is a deadly set for raccoons and foxes; it is but little less effective in trapping for opossums, weasels, and minks.

When using baits, place them far back beneath overhanging banks, in hollow logs and stumps, in openings in drifts, beside logs, and at the bases of clumps of briers or sprouts. Keep them half-hidden by partly covering them with dead leaves, rotten wood, pieces of bark, dead grass, and the like. They should appear as if they had been partly buried by some animal. Baits placed in this manner stir the curiosity of passing animals and arouse far less suspicion than those that are placed out in the open.

In looking for good places to set traps, notice where paths pass between trees, logs, rocks, or stumps, or where trails run alongside logs or under arched roots or overhanging banks. Look for bridges or culverts, floodgates, tile outlets, hollow logs and trees, drifts and brush heaps. Not infrequently an old unused building in some remote pasture or meadow will prove to be a very valuable find to the trapper. Do not overlook any place of promise, for sometimes the less promising places will be of greatest value in producing catches.

Chapter VIII

Laying Out the Trap Line

After you have thoroughly prospected your trapping ground and have drawn a map of it on which you have indicated the best trapping places, the next procedure is to lay out the trap line, provided, of course, the season for lawful trapping is at hand and there has been sufficient cold weather to produce good fur. It is common practice for two trappers to work together, each operating on his own trap line, but both working together as partners in all other respects. The catch, of course, is jointly owned property. And it might be well to say a few words here about choosing the trapping partner. Get a good one—seasoned, if possible; industrious and amiable, if inexperienced. If you are unable to find the sort of partner you want, then do without. But if you have a partner, the two of you can often work together to advantage in laying out your trap lines.

Spread out the map you have drawn of the trapping grounds and see if you cannot figure out the best route to follow in establishing your line of traps. You will want it to pass through or near as many good trapping areas as possible. These can pretty well be determined by the indications you have made on your map of the locations of such things as dens, tracks, trails, feeding grounds, thickets, swamps, hills, marshes, streams, and the like. Choosing the best route ought not be a very difficult matter after you have closely studied the indications on the map.

GENERAL POINTS TO CONSIDER

Aside from touching as many good trapping spots as possible, the trap line should pass through the wilder portions of an area, following the courses of streams and valleys, clinging to lake shores or skirting ranges of hills. It should pass near available springs, sweep along the edges of swamps, enter deep woods, thread rocky canyons, and follow old, unused, backwoods roads. Old pastures and meadows are fine things to have in the vicinity of the trap line; as are clearings and old slashings.

Wind and weather should receive some consideration in choosing the general course of the trap line, particularly when trapping in wilderness sections. Wind can cause a lot of trouble in countries where snows drift badly; and heavy rains are a nuisance when streams are kept at flood stage for weeks at a time. It is a good idea to lay out the trap lines so that they will parallel as much as possible the direction of the prevailing winds. And see that they do not cross any large streams that might offer trouble in case of floods. Where snows drift to great depths, avoid laying out the trap line in gulches and canyons that lie at right angles to the direction of the prevailing winds. Sheltered thickets and woods are good places to trap in those sections where deep snows are common.

LAY OUT TRAP LINES IN LOOPS OR CIRCLES

After one has determined the general course of the trap line, one should study the detailed map of the area to see how the line may be laid out to best advantage. If one is working out of a main camp, the best plan, no doubt, is to have the trap line in a circle or loop. Often an elongated loop is best. Even when overnight camps are used, there is usually some advantage in having the line in the form of a circle or loop. Of course, this does not preclude the idea of branching out with small loops at various points on the main line. This may often be done to reach some section particularly rich in fur game, or to enable one to trap some stream or lake shore where there are numerous signs or tracks. It is obvious, of course, that all trapping grounds have their good spots and their poor areas. The main idea when establishing a route for the trap line is to cover as much good trapping territory as possible.

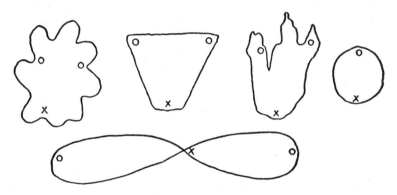

X - MARKS THE LOCATION OF THE TRAPPER'S CABIN
O- LONG LINES USE OVERNIGHT CAMPS

Various Methods of Laying Out a Trap Line.

It might be well to say here that the foregoing advice cannot always be followed to the letter, particularly when trapping in farming communities. Sometimes the signs and tracks of fur game appear in rather straggling formations at widely separated points on the trapping grounds. In order to reach as many good trapping places as possible, it then often becomes necessary to forget all about the general outline of the trap line and set traps at the most favorable locations. Under such circumstances, the course of one's trap line may ofttimes very much resemble the wanderings of a skunk or mink. But what does it matter? Perhaps more hours will be spent in tending one's traps; but of what consideration is this, when one knows one is trapping the best available places?

"Spot Trapping" a Territory

Where the signs and tracks of fur-bearing animals in a given area appear mostly in widely scattered places, it is often a good plan to do "spot trapping" there. But even when doing this sort of trapping one will do well to plan a general course for the trap line, with the idea of covering the most good trapping spots with the least effort. Many steps may often be saved by a little planning. Short cuts and straight lines can often mean the difference between utter weariness and just plain tiredness at the end of the day. Such planning is of course more important when trapping on foot than when trapping on horseback or by automobile.

Spot trapping requires no little keenness in locating the haunts of fur-bearing animals. Since only the best places in a given area are trapped, it becomes necessary to find these and use every advantage in trapping them. In this sort of trapping, one should use such sets as will not arouse the suspicions of animals; and there should be as little tracking about as possible. Trail sets and blind sets may frequently be used to good advantage in spot trapping. Bait sets may be used sparingly, too. Once an animal is so frightened that it leaves the area, the chances of again having the opportunity of trapping for it are indeed not promising; it will most likely never return to that spot. So it behooves the trapper to use the utmost care in setting and tending his traps. One should trap such places as if each night was going to be his only opportunity of capturing the fur-bearing animals found there.

Use of Maps and Notebooks in Laying Out the Trap Line

The use of maps and notebooks in laying out the trap line will often enable one to take advantage of many trapping opportunities that might otherwise be missed.

Working without a notebook or rather detailed map of an area, one may be setting traps within a short distance of a feeding ground or collection of dens without knowing it. There may be springs, tiny swamps, drifts, den trees, hollow logs and stumps in an area when one is utterly unaware of their presence. Mink may be using along a tiny spring-fed stream that the trapper knows nothing about; or a colony of skunks may occupy dens on a hillside where one had located them earlier in the season but had forgotten them. Muskrat colonies that were found earlier in the season and forgotten may occupy many places along a creek. All such information must be remembered to be of any value to the trapper; and the best way of keeping track of such data is to set down notes in a note-book and transfer their indications to a working map of the area to be trapped. Never trust too much to memory. Get it down in writing, or indicate it on a map. Then you will have something permanent on which to build.

Chapter IX

Set Locations

One of the first things the trapper looks for when exploring new territory is set locations. They commonly are the determining factor in the laying out of trap lines, especially when these occupy areas in farming communities. Eventually a trap line is thus established. More trap lines come into being in this manner than are deliberately laid out over certain routes.

Nothing is of greater importance in trapping than the locating of good places to set traps. It is usually the trappers who have a wide knowledge of animal habits and peculiarities that are good at locating these favorable places.

WHERE TO LOOK FOR GOOD SET LOCATIONS

Good set locations may often be found around drifts, in old pastures and about thickets, along streams, in hilly, rocky places, around the edges of swamps, and deep in the woods where there are many small areas of heavy undergrowth. One often will find them at places where there are snags, logs, or much driftwood in a stream; along the base of a high rock cliff is not a bad place to look for them; old fence rows usually have them in plenty; briery hillsides and deep gullies are often rich fields in which to search for them; and swamps, marshes, and boggy places frequently have plenty of trails and feeding places where good sets may be made. The finding of good places for setting traps is largely a matter of searching them out among the many and varied features of the physical characteristics of the area where one expects to do one's trapping.

More set locations will be found along streams and in the woods than in places where there is not a great amount of cover. Briery fence rows in the vicinity of deep woods or thickets are commonly better places to find set locations than along the fence rows in open farming country. Animals like plenty of cover. They like to use and travel in such places. They follow streams; use about thickets and woods; crawl around through drifts, brush heaps, hollow logs, and flag beds and tile outlets. They like to get in close places— holes in trees and rocks; openings in drifts, floodgates, and beneath culverts or bridges; and crevices among rocks at riffles or along the foot of rock cliffs. These are some of the better places to look for good set locations.

NATURAL SET LOCATIONS

There are hundreds of them on almost any trap line. Perhaps many times you have been walking along a footpath through a swampy area when you came upon a place where a sapling lay at right angles across it at the-height of four or five inches. This is a natural set location. Lay a small chunk of wood at each side of the trail where it passes beneath the sapling; set your trap in a shallow depression in the trail at this point, covering it very carefully; and you have made a most killing set at a very favorable natural set location. It is as simple as that, once you have found the right location. Train your eyes to look for all sorts of nooks and niches where animals travel. Don't overlook anything which may prove valuable as a location for a set. Too much can hardly be said about keeping the mind alert to the possibilities of such natural set locations as one may readily find when visiting traps.

Artificial Set Locations

When prospecting a place or tending traps, one sometimes finds places where fur game is using, but where there are no natural set locations. Quite often one will find places where animals have been traveling along a stretch of stream where high banks come down almost to the very edge of the water; or perhaps one will find a place in the open woods where fur game has been traveling from one pond to another, or from a group of dens to a feeding ground. There may not be any trail or well-marked course of travel at such places—just scattered tracks in the open to prove that animals have been using there. These are good places for making artificial set locations. Many such spots occur at various points on most trap lines.

Set Locations—Artificial Set Location at Left—Bait Set at Right.

Artificial sets are made in various ways. Almost any sort of place will be suitable for them, provided the right type of set is used. Where animals have been traveling at the foot of a high bank, one can make a set anywhere along the line of travel and lean a piece of bark, long, flat stone, stick, or other suitable object at an angle against the acclivity. This forms an opening through which animals will pass. Such a location makes an excellent set. Or one can place two small logs near each other where animals are traveling and set a trap at one end of the passageway thus created; or a trap may be set at each end. Good artificial set locations may be made by leaning a heavy stick against a tree, by bridging small streams with light logs, or by excavating a shallow tunnel beneath a fence. One of the best set locations I have ever used may be made by stacking up rock fragments in the form of a rough wall at or near a rock outcropping, leaving an opening through which animals may pass. Or one may lay some coarse brush against the abutment of a culvert, partly blocking the path of any animal that might be passing that way. An observant trapper will have no difficulty in finding many places on his trap line where artificial sets may be used to good advantage.

Set Locations in Relation to the Surroundings

Some sets are far more successful than others of the same kind. Sometimes this is because more animals are using about the successful sets; but not always is this true. The position and character of the set in relation to the surroundings often has much to do with its efficiency as a game-getter. Animals have certain routes of travel, special spots where they frequent. If sets are located near such places, they naturally are going to take more animals than sets occupying places where fur game is not traveling much. Then again, sets made in the vicinity of dens or feeding grounds have a better chance of catching animals than those located at points remote from such places. If there is much cover near a set, or if a set is well hidden among rocks or bushes, it will have a better chance of making catches. Sets made in the open, without natural attractions about them, seldom catch much fur game.

Chapter X

Making Sets

If any one thing in trapping is of greater importance than others, it is the making of good sets. Even if one has the ability to find where fur game is using and to read the signs and tracks readily, if one is unable to make good sets, one can never hope to be much of a trapper. In fact, if there is a key to successful trapping, I would say it is the ability to make good sets.

After the trapping ground has been prospected and places for setting traps have been found, the task of making sets will be the next thing to claim the trapper's attention. Inexperienced or careless trappers are inclined to overlook many of their opportunities when it comes to this sort of work. It is so easy to slap a trap down any old place without regard to positioning it, or with little or no thought given to the material needed for covering it or how this material is to be used. Professional trappers seldom make such mistakes. They look over the situation at a set location, figure out everything to be needed and how to go about their work, then begin making the set. They know beforehand just where they will position the trap, what sort of covering material will work best at this particular set, and just how they will fasten the trap. In short, they have planned the set in every detail before beginning work on it.

Keep Surroundings Natural

Nothing will mess up a set more disastrously than undue disturbance of the surroundings. Tramping about the set location is bad; littering the place with whittlings, broken sticks, spilled tobacco or the stubs of cigarettes is worse; or digging about the spot and converting it into a shambles of all sorts of rubbish is still worse. A set location when finished should not show any signs of disturbance of the surroundings; everything in the vicinity of the trap should look as natural as before the trap was set. In fact, one should be able to step back from a good set and never know by the looks of the surroundings that a trap is hidden there.

When you approach a place to make a set, look everything over carefully at a short distance and determine just where you will place the trap, how you will cover it, and what sort of trap fastening you will use. Be sure to have everything at hand that you will need in making the set, so that you will not have to be tramping in and out to get needed articles. If it is necessary to make any sort of excavation for the trap or bait, throw the dirt you remove to some little distance from the set location. Do not move things more than is absolutely necessary. Anything that has to be moved should be replaced carefully when the set is finished, being sure to efface all signs of disturbance. Drags or clogs can be made to appear natural by sifting a few dry leaves over them, or by throwing a few wisps of dry grass across them; be sure to use whichever sort of covering fits in well with the surroundings. See that the trap is covered with the same material that surrounds it. And as you back away from the finished set, be sure to obliterate any disturbance you have made, such as brushing out your tracks, straightening broken weeds, and the like.

Kinds of Sets

Broadly speaking, there are three classes of sets—water sets, land sets, and snow sets. A fourth might be included—under ice sets, which are nothing more than water sets made beneath the ice. This classification may still be divided into blind sets, bait sets, trail sets, and den sets. To the uninitiated trapper, this may seem like a rather formidable array of sets; but the fact is, they are all. patterned very closely after a single type of set. They take their names mostly from the locations where the trap is set and whether or not bait is used in connection with the set.

Much has been written about the blind set. Some confuse it with the trail set. However, it is a distinct type of set, being in a few outstanding respects entirely different to any other set. It is made like any other set, except that it is located where there are no signs to show that any animal has ever passed that way. It may be made in snow, on land, or under water. Its location is determined entirely by the surroundings, which should always be such as to cause the trapper to think that any animal passing near would be likely to travel over the spot where the trap is set. Thorough knowledge of animal habits and peculiarities are needed to enable one to make good blind sets.

Bait sets are just what their name applies—sets that require baits for luring animals to the traps. They may be used at almost any location, but are at their best when they are placed in secluded nooks, where the baits may be partly hidden. They should always be placed where signs show that animals have been using. Quite often sets of this nature are made in the vicinity of trails, dens, and at blind set locations.

Trail sets are perhaps used more widely than any other type of set. They are made simply by setting traps in trails, runways, or other places where tracks show that animals have been running. They can be land sets, snow sets, or water sets. Where the trails are wide—two or three times the width of a steel trap—they may be narrowed down by placing rocks or chunks of wood so as to confine the animals to a line of travel not much wider than the trap. Not infrequently narrow places in a trail can be found, usually where the line of travel passes between trees, logs, or other natural objects. Such places make better set locations than those where the trail has to be narrowed down by artificial means. Trail sets are usually very effective, and when properly made, can nearly always be depended upon to take game.

Now we come to the oldest type of set—the den set. This set is the mainstay of most beginning trappers. It is a very effective set when properly made, but has the bad features of being easily found by trap pilferers and of scaring away fur game by the catches creating a disturbance at the entrance to the den. This latter objection may often be partly eliminated by fastening the traps to drags or clogs, so that an animal, when caught, may be enabled to leave the vicinity of the den. However, it is poor policy to group den sets, since such practice has a tendency to frighten away fur game from a locality.

Den Set—Left. Runway Set—Right.

There are other special types of set, such as the dirt-hole set, the spring set, the chaff-bed set, the hollow-log set, and the like. It is scarcely worth while, however, to discuss these, since most of them are merely modifications of some one or more standard sets.

MAKING THE SET

When it comes to the actual work of making the set, a few words of explanation and advice may be worth something, especially to the beginning trappers, who will often find the task rather strange and novel.

After one has decided on the exact location for the trap, the first thing to be done is to scoop out a shallow depression in which to place it. This depression should be such that the trap will fit into it not too snugly, and ought to be only of such depth as to bring the trap pan on a level with the surrounding soil. If a long-spring type of trap is to be used, be sure to make a depression for the spring, too, which will be turned at an angle of forty-five degrees toward the fixed trap jaw. Line this depression with dry dead leaves, dry grass, cattail fluff, or other soft, dry substances of like nature. This will not only cushion the trap, but will prevent the set from freezing up in cold weather.

In making the set, always plan to place the trap with its bed plate parallel with the animal's line of travel. This will result in the animal stepping on the trap pan from one end of the trap. Never set the trap so that an animal will have to step over a trap jaw. Such a setting is likely to result in the trap turning or tilting, especially if the animal fails to set its foot exactly in the middle of the trap pan. Then, too, such a setting may result in the animal's foot being thrown clear of the jaws when the trap snaps shut.

COVERING AND FASTENING THE TRAP

In general, the materials used to cover the trap should be such as to conform well with the surroundings. Traps set at locations where there are dead leaves, should be covered with dead leaves; traps set where there is dry grass, should be covered with dry grass; traps set on the muddy bottoms of streams should have a covering of mud-smeared leaves; and snow sets should have the traps covered with snow, brushing it down with an evergreen branch to smooth it. The main thing to remember in placing such coverings is to have them smooth and natural looking. Traps should not be covered too heavy or too light. Just enough covering to hide the trap is sufficient.

When using snow or dirt for covering material, most trappers brush it out lightly with an evergreen branch. Leaves should be flat and flexible, or slightly powdered, and should cover the trap smoothly. Powdered rotten wood, dry dirt or dust, moss, and powdered dry leaves, all make good covering material when they conform with the surroundings. When using snow, finely pulverized rotten wood, or dirt or sand for covering the trap, it is a good plan to place a piece of paper on the trap pan. This paper should be cut to fit nicely within the spread jaws of the trap. Otherwise, such materials are likely to sift beneath the trap pan and clog the action of the trap.

Wire fastenings are good, if a tough wire of good quality, suitable size, and sufficient strength is used. The wire should be the size of baling wire or larger, and needs to be at least five to six feet long. Short wires kink and break too easily. Be sure the wire is fastened securely at each end. Such wires are not needed when fastening traps to drags or drowning devices. However, be sure the swivels on the trap chains work freely, for no sort of trap fastening is much good if the swivel is not working.

Many trappers use trap fastenings of insufficient length, especially when securing the trap to a fixed object. Here is where the use of an extension chain pays off. Use a generous length, fastening it to the regular chain with an "S" link, and forget about animals pulling out of traps. The standard length of trap chain will give satisfactory results in most instances, but for some sets, and when used under certain conditions, they are not of sufficient length.

Drowning Stakes in Use. Trap at the Left—Tile Set. Trap at the Right—
Bank Set.

The only places I can think of where a stake or fixed object might be used to advantage are where a trap is set at the edge of deep water with a drowning stake close by or where two traps are placed within a few inches of each other with the idea of stretching out a catch so as to prevent its twisting off a foot or gnawing out of the trap. However, it is a good rule always to fasten the trap in such a manner as to permit some movement of it when the captured animal struggles to escape.

ANTICIPATE COMING WEATHER CONDITIONS

Weather governs to no little extent the choice of set to be used. It would be useless to make a snow set at a time when all indications pointed to a big thaw within a few hours; or to make a water set at the edge of a stream that was rising or falling rapidly; or to make a blind set in a sandy location in extremely windy weather; or to use bait sets when the weather was so cold that baits would be frozen solid in a short time after they had been placed. The weather often is a good partner to the trapper; and just as often it is anything but co-operative.

When indications point to a big snow in the offing, one will do well when making sets to keep away from deep gullies, exposed places, and all unprotected spots. Likewise, when the temperature is fast dropping and broadcasting stations are sending out warnings of the coming of a prolonged heavy freeze, keep away from still, open waters when making sets. Heavy rains and slushy snows can make bad trapping in swamps or lowlands; dry, windy weather can cause one no little trouble when trapping in sandy or exposed locations; freezing weather often makes trapping something of a headache; and heavy, drifting snows are nearly always a nuisance when trapping in open sections where there is little or no protection for the sets. So try to anticipate coming weather conditions when setting traps.

Chapter XI

Mobile Trapping

Elsewhere in this book mention was made of using the automobile and the boat in trapping. Here we will go a little deeper into this subject. We will also discuss a few other methods of getting about on the trap line. Generally speaking, hoofing it is the ideal way to trap, but it is not always the best way. Sometimes it becomes desirable to mobilize the trapping operations in other ways.

Use of the Automobile in Trapping

Under certain favorable circumstances, the use of an automobile in trapping pays well. One reason for this is that the automobile permits the trapper to cover long trap lines without a great deal of effort. Not infrequently the auto trapper will lay out a trap line one hundred miles or more in extent. Another reason is that the trapper can cover the most favorable territory, skipping the less promising places. He can trap such places as roads following rivers, or such locations as mountain valleys, lake shores, or large creeks. Too, he has great opportunity for doing "spot trapping," touching only the most favorable "fur pockets" in a wide territory.

The selection of the right automobile for trapping is worth a little thought. Most well-known makes are nowadays good enough for this use—Ford, Chevrolet, Dodge, Jeep. Perhaps the Jeep is somewhat better adapted to roughing it than some of the others. But it is the way the car is equipped that really counts. See that there are snow tires on the rear wheels, that there is plenty of room inside the body and in the trunk for storing equipment, that there is good road clearance, and that there are tire chains if the vehicle has smooth tires. Many trappers use pick-up trucks, but a good used automobile is quite satisfactory. However, don't get an old crippled jalopy. Time is money to the trapper, and wasting time trying to get an old dilapidated car to run is certainly ruinous to a trapper's income. See that the car has a good engine, transmission, differential, and tires that can be depended upon to take you there and get you back. Good used cars nowadays can be bought for a few hundred dollars and will soon pay for themselves on the trap line. One caution is worth considering: keep the gasoline level above the halfway mark in the tank at all times.

An auto trapper will need to carry some extra parts and other items of equipment for emergency use. These will include distributor points, spark plugs, a can of motor oil, an extra gallon of antifreeze, a gallon of gasoline, a tow chain, a squirt oil can, a jack, tools for working on the car, and extra links for the tire chains. It is not a bad idea to carry a good axe and a shovel. And don't forget an extra wheel with pumped tire in place.

In using the automobile on the trap line, it is a good idea to carry extra clothing—raincoat, heavy jacket, and the like—so as to be ready at all times for sudden changes of weather. Too, a small amount of food that needs no or little preparation will often come in handy. And here is a little trick that one will do well to remember. The auto trapper can always have fire, even if he is out of matches, just by soaking a piece of rag in gasoline and holding it to a spark plug that has been removed from the cylinder head but that still has the wire attached. He can then place the plug on the cylinder head and start the engine. The resulting spark will ignite the gasoline-soaked rag.

In nearly all sections of the country there are good hard roads—concrete, macadamized, blacktop—following the shores of lakes, or the courses of rivers or creeks. Such places are the bread and meat of the auto trapper. He should work all such places well, keeping in mind the advantages to be gained in doing "spot trapping." Streamlets along the roads or highways, culverts, rock cliffs, swamps, thickets—all offer good opportunities to the person who wants to use the automobile in his trapping. And he shouldn't forget the back-country dirt roads, for these are perhaps the best places of all to trap, especially in dry weather. However, the traveled highways often provide good trapping to the person who cares to go after it.

Trapping may also be done from a motor coach or house trailer. These vehicles are used mostly as base camps, and are moved from place to place as trapping requirements dictate. They give one a mobile home from which trapping may be done. One can trap from a boat which has been carried on top of the motor coach or trailer, from a bicycle or light motorcycle carried along as a part of the equipment, or on foot. When choosing the motor coach or house trailer, it is advisable to select one that is sturdy but comparatively light, compact, and no larger than is needed. There are many makes, all practical. Choice is merely a matter of finding one with inside fixtures that best meet one's needs. One can be a little more liberal in choice of equipment for such a vehicle, since space requirements are not so restricted. Practically the same sort of outfit will be needed, except more food supplies can be carried. These should be concentrated and easily prepared foods, such as quick oats, minute rice, powdered milk, and instant mashed potatoes. These are a godsend to the trapper who has to prepare his own meals. One will also find more room here for traps, fur stretchers, and other trapping equipment.

It is always something of a problem to know just how to care for the catch when living in a motor coach or a house trailer. Raw furs need plenty of air while curing, and air circulation should be good. Neither of these is found in the mobile home, be it motor coach or house trailer. Some trappers get around this problem by carrying a small, well-ventilated tent; others use a portable knock-down fur shed. Even so, this situation constitutes one of the drawbacks of this type of trapping.

Trapping by Rowboat and Motorboat

The description of a good trapping boat, together with directions for building it, may be found elsewhere in this book, so here we will discuss mostly the conveniences and uses of the rowboat and motorboat in trapping.

There are many kinds of rowboats in use today. They are made of various materials, such as steel, galvanized metal, fiberglass, aluminum, and wood. All have their good points. However, a sturdy, light, wood rowboat is hard to beat. Such a boat, if cared for properly, will serve the trapper well over a period of many years.

One of the great advantages in using the rowboat is the ease with which the trapper can put out his traps, and the fact that sets can readily be made without disturbing the surroundings. If one carries a paddle in addition to the oars, one can creep slowly along the shore at inlets and shallow coves—where fur game is often found—with no paddling difficulty. If the boat has a hinged locker beneath the back and center seats, there will be no trouble in carrying needed trapping supplies, such as traps, wire for use as trap fasteners, trap stakes, trap setters, and extra trap chains. Moreover, such an arrangement eliminates the inconvenience of having these articles underfoot on the boat bottom.

Another decided help in boat trapping is that of being able to tend one's traps easily and regularly without slogging along the shore, perhaps on ice or through deep snow or mud. Then, too, one can get the catch back to camp without great effort.

Perhaps most motorboats used by trappers are rowboats equipped with outboard motors. There are many such motors—Johnston, Evenrude, Mercury, and a whole host of others. They are made in several sizes and types. One should choose a well-known make of three to five horsepower, and equip it with a safety chain. The chain is important. I have recently seen three outboard motors lost—in twenty to fifty feet of water—because of the clamps working loose.

A motorboat makes work easy for the lake or river trapper. Such a boat permits the trapper to tend longer trap lines, and gives him an advantage over the trapper on foot in reaching difficult set locations. When used in connection with a motor coach or a house trailer, the trapper is just about "king" of the lakes and rivers. He can move along from place to place, trapping the best locations and passing up those not so good. In this manner, he can trap a wide section, getting the cream of the trapping, then move on quickly to new territory with the minimum of inconvenience.

THE USE OF BICYCLES AND MOTORCYCLES IN TRAPPING

The bicycle to be used in trapping should be selected with great care. In choosing one, see that the frame is strong and well made, the seat comfortable and easily adjustable, the tires of good quality, and the chain well protected by a full-length guard. One's best guarantee of these features is to select a well-known make from a reliable dealer. Once the machine is in use, regularly check the wheel bearings, pedal bearings, crank bearings, brake, and wheel alignment. It is a good idea, also, to occasionally check the steering head bearings, and the chain for proper tension. These parts should have attention every few hundred miles. Remember that the life of the bicycle is determined by such inspections, plus careful use and proper lubrication.

When using the bicycle as a means of getting about, the trapper should plan his trap line so that it will be in an oval or circular form. In this way he will not have to double back on any part of his line; neither will he find any long stretches barren of sets. He should keep to good roads or well-traveled trails—the bicycle was not made for use in the woods or thickets. A parcel carrier on the handle bar and another at the rear of the machine will be handy for carrying traps, trap wire, baits, and the like. A good bicycle lock will come in handy, since the trapper will be away from his machine much of the time.

Motorcycle trapping has many advantages over trapping with an automobile. A motorcycle can be driven over woodland trails, along fire lanes, across small streams, through fields—places where an automobile would stall, choke down, and stop going. Too, it can be easily loaded into a boat, on the bumper of a car, or hauled around on a motor coach or house car, which greatly widens its sphere of usefulness. And no form of transportation—except the bicycle—is more economical.

Get a light machine. A heavy machine is more costly, mires more easily in mud or sand, and its only advantage over the lighter makes is that it is more powerful—and power alone will not get one out of a sand pit or a mud hole. Some very good makes of the lighter motorcycles and motorbikes are the Harley-Davidson M-65, the Honda, the Riverside Sport Bike, any of the Riverside light motorcycles, and the Bridgestone. These makes will give excellent service, even when used on the roughest trails.

Equip your motorcycle with sturdy luggage carriers or spacious saddle bags, and you are well fixed for trapping, even along the back trails, rugged though they may be.

Trap Uncovered.

Chapter XII

Natural and Artificial Lures

There is some controversy among trappers about the necessity or advisability of using natural or artificial lures in trapping. Some maintain that in making sets the traps should be carefully concealed, and nothing should be added that might cause an animal to think there could be something unusual at that spot. Others say that by making use of lures many catches will be made by thus attracting the animals to the vicinity of the sets. Be this as it may, many modern trappers use lures—and swear by them.

Generally speaking, the object of using lures is to attract the animal to the vicinity of the set, then to keep it interested in the bait, scent, or lure until it gets its foot on the pan of the trap. Of course, lures should be used judiciously. There are times when a certain lure may increase one's chances of making a catch twentyfold; at other times and other sets its effectiveness may be almost zero; and sometimes a set will be far more effective without bait or lure.

There are many kinds of lures. And they are used for many purposes. Some lures are used to arouse the curosity of an animal; some are used to appeal to the animal's appetite; some arouse the animal's passion; and some attract animals by the sense of smell alone, fooling them into the belief that other animals of their kind have been in the vicinity. Lures are good attractors, but they need human brains in applying them correctly to trapping needs.

CURIOSITY LURES

Such lures as these are commonly used in trapping for foxes and raccoons, although other animals may at times be taken in sets where they are in use.

One of the best curiosity lures is the bright metal lure. Cut a piece of tin, aluminum, tinfoil, or other bright metal in the shape of a small fish and fasten it to the pan of the trap. Make the set in shallow water at the shore of a clear stream, covering the trap carefully with water-soaked leaves. (Of course the bright lure is left uncovered.) This is a killing set for raccoons. Small pieces of mussel shell or china will work equally well.

A very good set for raccoons is what I call the "tin can set." Tie a long string to a bright tin can and fasten it to a low limb of a tree or bush in such a manner that the can will swing a foot or more above the ground. Swaying slightly in a light breeze, such an object will be investigated by any raccoon passing near it. A piece of glass or a small mirror may be used in place of the tin can.

The fox is an animal whose curiosity is easily excited. He will examine almost anything that is a little unusual. One of the best curiosity lures for taking this animal is nothing more than a strip of white cloth fastened to a stick about two feet above the ground and placed some ten or fifteen feet from a large ant hill or similar dirt mound. Set the trap on the mound, carefully concealing it with whatever material is found at the set. Any fox passing such a set is sure to circle the "flag," and in doing so will invariably get upon the dirt mound, where it is almost sure to step in the trap.

Oil of rue, cumin, or oil of asafetida makes a powerful artificial curiosity lure for use in trapping raccoons and foxes.

FOOD BAITS

Food baits are one of the oldest and most effective trapping lures known. Each species of animal has its favorite foods—bears like fruits and honey; minks are partial to small birds and fish; raccoons love berries and mussels; skunks eat birds' eggs and grubs; and weasels like live foods, such as rabbits and birds. If a trapper uses a suitable bait, any hungry fur-bearer will be attracted to the set. And if the bait is partly hidden, as if it were the leavings of a former meal of some animal, a catch is fairly certain. Baits of this type have both eye and nose appeal.

Here are some favorite foods of various species of animals: Muskrats—carrots, parsnips, fish, flag root, and mussel meat. Raccoons—wild grapes, poke-berries, fish, small birds, frogs, mussel meat, and persimmons. Foxes—mice, rabbits, small birds, poultry, eggs, burnt cracklings, and partly decayed fish. Minks—fish, small birds, muskrat meat, and poultry. Skunks—grubs, birds, roots, berries, and birds' eggs. The weasel likes to kill its foods, which consist mainly of rabbits, birds, poultry, and all kinds of small game.

SCENTS AND ALLIED LURES

This type of lure appeals to an animal's sense of smell. Such a lure, when properly used, is very effective. However, it should be used sparingly rather than profusely. If too much is used at a set, there is a tendency to arouse suspicion rather than to attract.

Most fur-bearing animals have scent glands. Extracts of these are used in compounding many of the natural lures. Pure extracts make very powerful lures, especially when used in trapping for the kind of animal from which the gland was taken. Scents made from glands and musk sacs of animals are often used without mixing with others. Again, they are frequently combined with others, several being compounded into a single lure. As a rule, this is a job for the regular lure manufacturer, since the average trapper cannot often do it right. Lure manufacturers commonly conduct many field tests of different lures, and are therefore in a better position to know how to combine scents for best results.

Beaver castors, muskrat musk glands, mink musk glands, fox scent glands, and the scent glands of the raccoon and the weasel are a few of the animal glands commonly used in making lures. Usually a base substance is used, such as fish oil, tonquin musk, etc., to properly blend the various ingredients, which makes the lure much more effective.

Animal droppings and urine make excellent lures. Any wild animal droppings or urine may be used; but to be most deadly, these lures should be the secretions from the kind of animal for which one is trapping. A good substitute for animal urine may be had by compounding such ingredients as ammonia, rain water, oil of carmel, and oil of asafetida. A few drops of urine or a small quantity of droppings are sufficient.

Fish oil makes an excellent lure for many of the fish-eating animals. It can be bought in drug stores, or may be readily made at home. The homemade product is far superior to the commercial oil. It is easily made by cutting up small fish in little pieces, placing them in a loosely corked, wide-mouthed bottle, and exposing them to the summer sun for three or four weeks. An oil will rise, which should be strained and kept in a bottle with a small neck. Place a few drops of this oil near the set.

A good fox lure is made by slowly boiling the cork-like formations found on the inside of a horse's foreleg. Boil for a couple of hours together with a piece of asafetida the size of a butter bean. A piece of the cork-like substance the size of a hickory nut will make almost a pint of lure. Smear this preparation about the set, but never on the trap. It will attract foxes from a long distance.

SOME FORMULAS FOR ARTIFICIAL LURES

Fox Lures—Tincture of asafetida, 5 drops; skunk scent, 3 drops; trout oil or fish oil, 4 ozs.; muskrat musk, 1/2 oz.; fox urine, 2 ozs. Age two months.

Eel oil, 4 ozs.; beaver castor, 1 oz.; muskrat musk, 1 oz.; skunk scent, 2 drops; tincture of asafetida, 4 drops. Age six weeks.

Weasel Lures—Fish oil, 4 ozs.; weasel musk, 2 ozs.; beaver castor, 1/2 oz.; rabbit blood, 2 ozs.; oil of anise, 6 drops. Age six weeks.

Sun-rendered trout oil, 4 ozs.; dried blood, 1/2 oz.; weasel musk, 2 ozs.; muskrat musk, 2 ozs.

Muskrat Lures—Fish oil, 2 ozs.; muskrat musk, 1/4 oz.; oil of sweet flag, 1/2 oz.; oil of sweet fennel, 10 drops; beaver castor extract, 1/2 oz.; oil of catnip, 10 drops. Blend well. Very effective.

Muskrat musk, 1 oz.; mink musk, 1/2 oz.; glycerine, 1/2 oz.; oil of anise, 10 drops.

Mink Lures—Sun-rendered trout oil, 4 ozs.; tincture of muskrat musk, 1 oz.; mink musk, 1/2 oz.; beaver castor, 1/2 oz.; oil of anise, 10 drops. Age two months.

Commercial or homemade fish oil, 2 ozs.; muskrat musk, 1/2 oz.; tincture of tonquin musk, 8 drops; mink musk, 1 oz. Good.

Raccoon Lures—Honey, 4 ozs.; beaver castor, ½ oz.; muskrat musk, ½ oz.; oil of anise, 20 drops.

Trout oil, 4 ozs.; strained honey, 4 ozs.; muskrat musk, 1 oz.; oil of anise, 1 oz.; tincture of tonquin musk, ½ oz.; extract of wild cherry, ½ oz. Age two months.

Opossum Lures—Fish oil, 4 ozs.; tincture of asafetida, 1 oz.; oil of lovage, ½ oz.; liquid camphor, 6 drops.

Trout oil, 2 ozs.; muskrat musk, ½ oz.; tonquin musk, 4 drops; oil of rhodium, 4 drops.

Skunk Lures—Oil of skunk flesh, 4 ozs.; fish oil, 2 ozs.; muskrat musk, 2 ozs.; tincture of asafetida, ½ oz.

Essence of skunk scent, 15 drops; melted cheese, 2 ozs.; fish oil, 4 ozs.; beaver castor, 2 ozs. Age six weeks.

Otter Lure—Salmon oil, 4 ozs.; beaver castor, 1 oz.; muskrat musk, 2 ozs.; mink musk, 2 ozs.

Coyote Lures—Trout oil, 4 ozs.; beaver castor, 1 oz.; asafetida, ¼ oz.; muskrat musk, 3 ozs.; skunk scent, 5 drops.

Coyote urine, 2 ozs.; sun-rendered fish oil, 4 ozs.; tincture of tonquin musk, 1 oz.; valerin, 8 drops; beaver castor, ½ oz.; skunk scent, 2 drops.

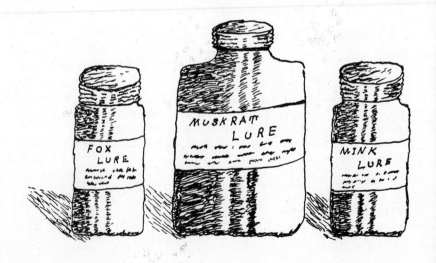

Chapter XIII

Trapping the Weasel

No animal of comparative size is more ferocious and blood-thirsty than this little carnivore, which is the smallest of the marten or weasel family. Feared by a host of small rodents and ground-nesting birds, it moves about the marshes, woods, and fields in quick, short jumps, always placing its feet side by side. This fearless little animal with elongated body, short powerful legs, and long stocky neck delights in killing, apparently just for the devilry of it. Unbelievably quick in its movements, it will pounce upon its victim, sinking its sharp teeth deep into the muscles of the throat to reach the jugular vein. It often attacks animals many times its own size, such as rabbits, muskrats, and woodchucks, and is very destructive to poultry. It is so ferocious and courageous that it will even attack the eagle.

The weasel commonly attains a length of seven to eleven or more inches, the male being slightly larger than the female. This animal brings forth each year two or, rarely, three litters of young, averaging four to seven to the litter. The young mature within twelve months, and often attain an age of eight to ten years. The natural enemies of this little fur-bearer are the fox, the great horned owl, the fisher, the lynx, and the mink.

It is said that there are thirty-six species and subspecies of the weasel in North America. Some of these are known as stoat, ferret, or ermine. However, such nicety of distinction is not necessary for one to know the weasel, since the two colors of the animal—brown and white—are the features of greatest importance to the trapper. Weasels are brown in the Central and Southern parts of the country, and throughout the Northern sections only in summer. In all Northern sections, the fur of this animal becomes a creamy white or a pure white in winter, with a black tip on the tail. However, in the extreme Southern parts of the country, it commonly remains a chestnut brown throughout the year. In the far north—where habitat and climatic conditions bring about some change in the weasel's size and in the color and length of its fur—the animal is known as the ermine.

RANGE AND HABITS

Weasels are found in practically all parts of North America, occurring perhaps as near the North Pole as any land animal. This animal is a most desirable fur-bearer in Alaska and the Arctic regions, since here in these cold countries its pure white fur is most valuable. It inhabits plains as well as mountainous sections; and it usually is found in plenty in low marshes and dense forests throughout its entire range. It is not strictly a wilderness animal, since it often may be found in farming communities, usually in thickets, around stone fences or walls, and often along the rocky banks of streams or in wooded, hilly sections. It is fairly well distributed throughout its range, although it is commonly found in greater numbers in those sections where its natural food supply is most abundant.

The prey of this animal consists mostly of rabbits, mice, rats, gophers, muskrats, squirrels, birds, moles, and poultry when it is available. In almost any region where there are plenty of field mice and rabbits, there usually will be many weasels using. One will find their tracks and signs about stone walls, bridge abutements, brush heaps, hollow logs and stumps, or along briery fence rows at the edge of woods. Old unused roads in the deep woods and rock ledges along cliffs are often visited by this animal.

Weasels do most of their hunting at night, although they may sometimes be seen running about in the daytime, especially in the deep, dark woods. Weather seems not to bother them a great deal, since they run at all times. It never gets too cold or snowy for weasels to travel. I have often seen them out in severe snowstorms when the temperature was far below zero.

It is said that the weasel can smell a bloody bait more than an eighth of a mile away. I do not doubt this statement, for I know the animal has a very good sense of smell. Not infrequently I have seen it ferret out its prey, much the same as does the hunting dog. It has keen eyesight, too, often noticing the movements of mice or ground squirrels several yards away. It climbs trees and kills squirrels, although most of its hunting activities take place on the ground, where it visits various crevices, rock piles, hollow logs, brush heaps, and the like. It not infrequently enters the dens of other animals, killing the inmates and sucking their blood.

PRACTICAL METHODS OF TRAPPING

Most trappers commonly trap the weasel at baited sets. Nearly anything in the way of bloody flesh will do for bait, although a freshly killed rabbit or the fresh carcass of a muskrat is to be preferred. The bloodier the bait, the better. Some few trappers use the blind set in trapping for this little fur-bearer; and it is a fairly successful set when used at the right locations, which are at crevices in rock piles or at the foot of rock cliffs, at openings in brush heaps or log heaps, at hollow logs, and around dry drifts in marshes or lowlands. Some use natural scents and artificial lures to capture this animal. And occasionally an animal is caught in a trap set in paths or runways. But by far the most catches are made at bait sets and blind sets.

Frequently weasels travel along certain routes when using in thickets and about lowlands. They often visit the same drifts, hollow logs, and brush heaps on these trips. Such places make excellent set locations. Where trails can be found, one may often use the trail set to very good advantage. Trails are not easily found, as a rule; but sometimes one may find where the animals have been traveling along fence rows or around bridge abutments, or even through openings in rock piles or rock fences or walls. Traps set at such places should be well concealed, since they are likely to catch other fur game. Holes under haystacks and straw-stacks are good places to set traps, too, for weasels are commonly attracted to such places by the innumerable mice that often harbor at them.

The No. 1 trap is the right size for weasel trapping, though many trappers prefer the No. 1½ size, claiming that the larger trap catches about the body and kills the victim, which is often true. Some few trappers use the wire rat trap for catching this animal. This trap is similar to the ordinary wire mouse trap, except that it is larger and stronger. It works quite well, but can hardly be recommended for general use. The common steel trap is best— either the long-spring trap or the underspring type. These traps can be used in more places, and will work well in nearly all sorts of weather.

VALUING WEASEL SKINS

The skin of the weasel being very tender, extreme care must be taken in skinning the animal, lest cuts or tears damage the pelt. Skinning should be done so as to produce a cased pelt. Remove the tail bone by splitting the skin part way down the tail and stripping the skin off with the thumb and forefinger. See that the ears are cut off very close to the skull, and that skinning about the eyes, nose, and mouth is carefully done. Stretch the skin on a thin stretcher of suitable size, being careful to have it on the board straight before pulling it down tight. All weasel pelts are stretched with the skin side out.

Weasel skins are valued according to size, quality, and the color of the fur. Pure white pelts are of the greatest value. Brown-furred pelts sell for much less money. Skins from northern sections are most valuable, as they are larger and have better fur.

Weasel Tracks—Animal Running.

Chapter XIV

How to Trap the Muskrat

This little water animal looks and acts much like a small beaver. So much so, in fact, that some of the Indian tribes always considered beavers to be only overgrown muskrats. Just how they accounted for the difference in the tails of the two animals is not clear. However, this is not such a glaring error as it might seem, since many of our early historians mistook this little fur-bearer for an overgrown water rat.

Muskrats are night-roving animals. They love to swim about shallow coves or to use along willow-fringed sections of a stream or pond, where they feed upon flag roots, water grasses, mussels, fish, and the like. Often they leave the water to make paths back to some corn field or turnip patch. They live in dens in the banks of streams, as well as in dome-shaped houses built of weeds, mud, grasses, reeds, and sticks, which are most frequently located in shallow water in marshes and ponds, often some distance from the shore. The entrance to these habitations is usually below the water surface. The dens are commonly found along those parts of a stream or pond where there is much willow growth, or where there are exposed roots of large trees that have been partly washed out.

The muskrat is an excellent diver and swimmer, having broad, webbed hind feet, and tiny ratlike front feet which it folds against its body when in motion in the water. Its long, scaly, oval-like tail is used as a rudder in swimming. This same long tail is often a means of identifying the tracks of this animal when seen in mud or snow, since its tip drags occasionally, leaving short, indistinct, linear marks between the tracks along the line of travel. The animal is very prolific, bringing forth six to ten young at a time, and sometimes having as many as three litters a year. Its range is wide, practically covering all the United States and most of Canada, even to the Arctic regions. Its chief enemies are the otter, mink, lynx, fisher, and the great horned owl.

This little fur-bearing animal differs considerably in size in the various parts of its range. Its fur, too, differs in value in many parts of the country. Muskrats in eastern Canada and the northeastern part of the United States are larger and better furred than in the western and southern parts of the country. Along the Atlantic Coast, in Connecticut, New York, Maryland, and Virginia, there is a black furred muskrat, the pelt of which commands extremely good prices. Farther south, in Alabama and Louisiana, the muskrat is somewhat smaller and has a light-brown fur, which is not so valuable. The fur of the muskrat is very like that of the beaver, except that it is shorter and somewhat less silky.

Best Muskrat Trapping Countries

Some of the best sections for trapping muskrats are found in the marshes lying adjacent to the Great Lakes and along the Saint Lawrence River. But there are others just as good along the Atlantic Coast, particularly in New York, New Jersey, Delaware, Maryland, and northern Virginia. Ohio, Indiana, Illinois, and Missouri have some good muskrat territory; while the marshes and lakes of Wisconsin and parts of Iowa have plenty of muskrats, too.

Parts of Mississippi, Alabama, and Louisiana have some excellent muskrat trapping grounds. But of course the skins of the animals from these sections are not of as good quality as those of muskrats trapped in sections farther north. However, trappers in these countries often make up the difference in the value of the skins in the number of muskrats caught, since some of these southern regions yield very good catches.

Muskrat marshes in many parts of the country are leased for trapping. Particularly is this true of the big marshes along the Atlantic Coast and in Louisiana. Not infrequently marsh owners let out trapping grounds to responsible parties on a share basis; and occasionally one hires trappers to make the catches. For these reasons, all good muskrat trapping sections are not particularly attractive to "outside" trappers, for not always are they able to locate "open" territory in these places.

Habits of the Muskrat

The muskrat is strictly a gregarious animal. It lives in colonies in swamps, marshes, and streams, and along the borders of sloughs, lakes, and ponds. While it is mostly nocturnal in its habits, it is sometimes seen swimming about or feeding in the daytime, usually early in the morning or late in the evening. One commonly has little or no trouble in locating a colony of these animals, for nearly always there are a number of trails on the stream bank near their dens. Then, too, the animals leave signs of their presence in the water and at the various places where they feed along the banks. Collections of small mussel shells and fragments of flag root at various places in the water are good indications that muskrats are using in the vicinity.

In swamps and marshes, where there is a great amount of moss or plant growth in the water, it is not an uncommon thing to find narrow, open waterways running in all directions, where the animals have established regular routes of travel. They use these routes in going to and from their feeding grounds, and in gathering materials to build their dome-shaped houses. If one will notice the flag beds in the vicinity of such places, one will find "cuttings" and root fragments. Sometimes these are in small heaps in the water; at other times one will see them floating about among the standing flag and cattail. Such places are visited almost nightly by the muskrats that go there to feed. It is usually no trouble to find numbers of excellent set locations at these feeding grounds.

Muskrats are vicious fighters among themselves. Toward spring the old males will often fight until the weakest animal is killed. At this season, a trapper will not infrequently find damaging scars on a pelt, showing that the animal had been badly injured in a terrible fight. Sometimes a trapped animal will be killed and its skin entirely ruined by being chewed by other muskrats, although the flesh of such animals is almost never eaten. In as much as this little fur-bearer sometimes has three litters of young during the summer, the latest litter is often brought forth very late in autumn. The animals of all such litters are known in the fur trade as "kits." Their fur is of little value, and it is a great waste to trap them. This is one reason why so many experienced trappers do not do much fall trapping for muskrats. They know that a "kit" taken in November and worth perhaps fifteen cents might well be worth two or three dollars if it were left to be trapped in late winter or early spring.

TRAPPING MUSKRATS

Muskrats are usually much easier to trap in late fall and early winter. They are most active at this time, and can often be taken quite easily in trail sets and at underwater den openings. Later in the season, when ice rims the streams and ponds, trapping them becomes more difficult. Locations that offered good trapping earlier in the season now may prove of little or no value, since ice formation along the shore prohibits the use of adequate sets. The trapper now has to rely largely on bait sets, den sets, and traps set at favorable places beneath the ice. However, he often finds his smaller catch more valuable than a larger fall catch would be, since the pelts of muskrats do not attain full value until the latter part of winter.

The No. 1 steel trap is the right size for trapping muskrats. When set in about two inches of water, it will nearly always catch the victim by a hind leg or foot. Very few muskrats so caught will escape, since the thick muscles and massed tenons of these parts will prevent breakage of bones or the twisting off of a foot. This trap is sufficiently strong to hold muskrats well, and is more convenient than larger sizes to carry about and set. Some use the No. 1½ trap, claiming that when a drowning pole or drowning wire is used the extra weight aids in pulling a captured animal into deep water. However, I never have been able to see any need for the heavier trap, since I have at no time ever experienced any difficulty in the use of the smaller trap. In fact, I have found that the smaller trap has its advantages, in that it can be set in narrow, close places, and is more easily concealed.

The number of traps needed for muskrat trapping will vary with the character of the trapping grounds and the kinds of trapping to be done—whether trapping by boat, by automobile, or on foot; or whether it is to be full-time trapping in wilderness sections or only part-time trapping in settled communities. The professional 'rat trapper who works each day from daylight to dark will often find use for possibly three or four hundred traps, especially if he is "working" a large marsh where signs are plentiful. The trapper who operates along rivers or smaller streams will probably seldom use more than a couple of hundred traps. If he uses a motorboat or an automobile, he might possibly find use for fifty more. The schoolboy or farm hand who does only part-time trapping will usually find fifty or sixty traps about all he will need. A lot of muskrat trapping is done on trap lines where traps are also set for other fur-bearers. Such trappers will often use less than a hundred traps for muskrat sets.

There are two general methods of trapping this animal. They are those used in marsh and swamp trapping, and those used in trapping for the animals along streams and at sloughs or ponds. The difference in the habits of the muskrat in these two environments is responsible for this dissimilarity in the methods used in trapping it. In marshes and swamps, muskrats commonly live in houses, going in and out of these habitations by means of underwater openings. They use largely in the water at such places, thus making it necessary to use many different types of den sets, bait sets, and water sets. On the other hand, the animals when living on streams, sloughs, and ponds often have their dens in the banks, sometimes with openings at or below the water and at other times with the den entrances above the water level. They quite frequently use much on the banks, often at the edge of the water but not infrequently up on land away from the water. Trail sets, den sets, and bait sets work well in trapping the animals at such places.

In places where the laws will permit such trapping, marsh and swamp trappers make many muskrat catches at sets made underwater at the entrance to the houses. Too, they get many 'rats at sets in trails or runs in shallow waters. A small trap of the underspring type, being flat and compact when set, will be found useful in making such sets. Bait sets are often used by swamp and marsh trappers where conditions are right for making them. A trap set in shallow water at a low grassy bank and baited with a few tiny cubes of parsnip, carrot, or turnip is almost certain to make a catch. Feeding grounds are also good places for locating sets. Muskrats often carry cuttings of grasses, cattail, and flag to some particular location at the feeding grounds, making small wisps or heaps of such material in the water. They often use these as resting places when eating. Such "tables" or resting places make fine locations for sets.

In many places in swamps and marshes, one will find narrow paths or runways in moss-beds or grass-beds. Traps set in these are almost certain to catch muskrats. Since the water at such places is often too shallow for the successful use of the drowning pole or drowning wire, some other certain method of drowning must be devised. In such instances, the trapper frequently uses stakes for drowning the catch. One stake is driven into the ground through the ring of the trap chain to serve as a fastening for the trap, while another stake is driven close by, allowing it to extend upward to or above the level of the water. When a muskrat is captured, it will swim around and around, winding the trap chain about the stake until the animal is pulled beneath the surface of the water and drowned. Sometimes drowning is effected by setting two traps only a few inches apart and stretching the chains out in opposite directions at full length before fastening them to stakes or other fixed objects. Even when a catch at such a set is not drowned, it will seldom escape, since the two traps stretch out the animal so as to make it impossible for it to twist off a foot.

A boat can often be used to good advantage in marsh and swamp trapping. In fact, one is frequently indispensable. See that it is a strong boat, light and wide, and well adapted for use in shallow places. A boat will be found most useful in reaching those muskrat houses way off yonder in open waters, as well as in nosing about the deeper channels and around feeding grounds and flag beds. Many a good set location that is out of reach for the trapper who wades in hip boots is readily approached by the one who operates from a boat. Nowadays, professional trappers quite frequently widen their sphere of operation by using a light motorboat.

In tidal marshes or inlets, where the water level is constantly changing, floating sets can frequently be used to good advantage. These are made by setting traps on floating chunks of wood or pieces of board that have been securely anchored to some fixed object in the water. The float should be well covered with water grasses; and the trap chain may be wired or otherwise fastened to the underside of it. Such sets may be baited, or, if suitably located, used without baits, as blind sets. Trappers who use scents and artificial baits will find that these can often be used to advantage in connection with these sets.

Stream, slough, and bayou trapping is sometimes a difficult proposition, especially in rainy seasons, when water levels are constantly changing. Floating sets will lessen the difficulty somewhat; but not all set locations are favorable for the use of this type of set. Not infrequently successful trapping under such conditions becomes largely a matter of calculation; that is, one's success then is determined largely by how accurate one can estimate the rise or fall of the water level during a given period, so as to have as many sets as possible in the proper depth of water and in good working order

Floating Set For Muskrats. Anchor log to a stake on the bank. Cover traps and log with shredded leaves of cattail. Place bait—small cubes of parsnip or carrot on top of the covering between the traps.

at that time during a night when the 'rats will be most active. In such circumstances, it is wise to have a few traps well set and in good operating condition rather than to have out a great number that cannot be expected to make catches. But in normal seasons, when the water level in the streams, sloughs, and bayous is fairly stable, such trapping can be a source of great pleasure and no little profit.

When trapping along streams or at the shores of sloughs or bayous, one will do well to watch for good places to set traps at the exposed roots around the bases of trees along the banks, at washed-out places under overhanging banks, at bank dens and "slides," at tile outlets and underwater den openings, beneath arched roots and at root wads, and at points where small streams empty into a slough, bayou, or larger stream. Quite often one will find places where the animals have been traveling in shallow water between a stick, chunk, or rock on the bank and deeper water out away from the bank. Sometimes the rock or chunk will be out in the water a few inches from the shore line. Either type of place is a sure bet for a water set. The drowning pole or drowning wire can be used to good advantage in connection with such sets.

Bait sets made along a bushy bank or at places where the willow-fringed shore dips down quickly to meet the water are commonly good game-getters. Set the trap in about two inches of water, and scatter half a dozen or so of tiny cubes of parsnip, carrot, or turnip near the set. Or traps set on logs or rocks at the edge of a stream will often make catches, even when no baits are used. All traps set for muskrats should be carefully covered, however, for one never knows when a mink or a raccoon may pass that way. Good muskrat sets may be made about drifts, floodgates, bridge abutments, and like places. Occasionally one will find an opening in an underground runway leading back to several bank dens. Not infrequently such runways have a couple of inches of water in them. No better place for a trap can be found. Set a trap in the runway and another one just outside the opening, staking each trap firmly. Such an arrangement of traps will prevent the captured animal from footing itself.

Preparing the Skins for Market

Muskrats should always be skinned so as to produce a cased pelt. This may be accomplished by using the knife to make an incision around the tail at its base and around each leg at the ankle, after which a slit is made from one hind foot down the inside of the leg, almost but not quite straight across the pelvic part of the body and up the other hind leg to the foot. Then a second incision is made from the center of this line to the root of the tail. The skin may now be pulled inside out over the carcass. Care must be taken not to tear the tender skin on the animal's belly, nor to cut the skin when working it off the animal's neck and head. Work very carefully around the ears, eyes, nose, and mouth. Cut off the ears next to the skull; and work the skin away from the eyes, nose, and mouth with the point of the skinning knife, using great care not to cut or mutilate the pelt. By slitting the skin across the body inside the hind legs rather than down the back of each hind leg—

as is the customary procedure when skinning animals to produce the ordinary cased skin—a longer back is produced, which is very desirable in muskrat pelts.

An easy, speedy way to skin a 'rat is to chop off the feet and tail with a sharp belt axe or hatchet, make the usual incisions, and pull the skin from the carcass. This method is not infrequently used by 'rat trappers in large marshes, where a great many muskrats must be handled each day. Generally wire fur stretchers are used for stretching these large catches. Since this type of stretcher permits a circulation of air about the fur side of the pelt, it is to be preferred when handling wet skins. Many trappers use the common board stretchers with blunt-pointed ends.

The skins of muskrats are graded as to size, primeness, and color. Thin, papery fall skins are of but little value. It is the red-pelted, heavy skins of late winter and early spring that bring the most money in the raw fur market. The darker-furred skins, too, are worth more than the lighter grayish-brown skins. Sometimes muskrat skins are sold "flat"; that is, at an average price for the lot. When a collection of skins does not have too many "kits" in it or too many pelts of small or fall-caught muskrats to make a wide variation in individual skin value, this is usually a very satisfactory way of buying and selling muskrat skins. At any rate, careful skinning and preciseness in stretching and curing will always pay big dividends. In fact, some trappers who work this way make almost as much money at the fur shed as they do on the trap line.

Muskrat Tracks in Mud—Animal Walking.

Chapter XV

Mink Trapping

To be able to set a trap for a mink and catch the animal within a reasonable length of time is the ambition of nearly every school-boy trapper. Young trappers and others without much trapping experience feel that they have become real trappers when they have gained such proficiency in making sets that they can regularly catch mink. Perhaps this conceit is due in a great measure to the popular idea that mink are such cunning and elusive fur-bearers that they can be caught only by experienced trappers who know certain secrets about mink trapping. The fact is, however, that mink are but little more difficult to trap than muskrats, if one will only make a study of their habits and use a little common sense in trapping them.

Mink are neither cunning nor elusive. However, they are some-what peculiar in some of their habits. Their ways of traveling about and hunting small birds and animals sometimes smack of slyness. They have a very keen sense of smell, which they use to good advantage in hunting for food. Like the weasel, the mink is a bloodthirsty killer, not infrequently killing apparently merely for the sport of it. This is especially true when the animal gets into a chicken coop or poultry house.

This animal is at home in nearly any locality where there are numerous waterways. It uses much about streams, lake shores, and in swamps and marshes, where it catches and kills rabbits, muskrats, small birds, fish, and frogs. In shape, it resembles the weasel, except that it is a somewhat larger animal, measuring often from twenty-eight to thirty-two inches in length. The fur of the mink is dark, with usually a small creamy-white spot or area under the animal's chin. The range of this animal is wide, comprising nearly all areas from the Gulf Coast in the United States to the Arctic Circle.

Mink are great wanderers. They not infrequently make runs of ten to thirty or more miles from their dens or homing grounds. One peculiarity of such travel is that they invariably visit the same spots when making these trips, going under exposed stump roots, through hollow logs, to tile outlets, and through openings in root wads and drifts. They will often travel runways in tiny spring-fed streams, or use around bridge abutments, and the like. They make such runs fairly regular, sometimes as often as every week or ten days. Not all mink, however, travel in this manner. Some remain in the vicinity of the spot where they were born, getting away occasionally only on short trips of a few miles. This animal seldom walks, but lopes about, taking jumps of around fifteen to twenty inches.

Haunts and Habits of Mink

Mink love to wander about in marshes and swamps, as well as along rivers, creeks, and small streams. They visit springs; and are often found in wooded, hilly sections, especially if these are threaded by a number of tiny spring-fed branches. Marshy lake shores are favorite haunts. And they often frequent farming communities, especially where these are near lakes, swamps, or streams. They are not infrequently abundant in mountainous sections where there are many small streams to supply them with an abundance of food.

Perhaps there are more mink around river and coast swamps and marshes and in bayou countries than in other parts, although some mountain streams have them in plenty. Wherever rabbits, small birds, muskrats, frogs, or fish are plentiful, one is quite likely to find the animals in fair numbers. Small creeks with an abundance of undergrowth along their banks are preferred haunts, as are grassy marshes with numerous frogs, small fish, and muskrats. In Southern sections, they are most abundant around bayous and swamps; in Northern sections, they are more often found around wooded lake shores and along swift, rocky streams.

Unlike the muskrat, the mink is a wide roamer. Tonight he may be wandering around in the maze of muskrat runways in a big swamp; tomorrow night he may be running a dashing stream on a mountainside ten or fifteen miles away. He likes to kill animals and birds for food, often sucking the blood of his victims and maybe eating only a small portion of the carcass. He visits every nook and spot along his route of travel, searching drifts, hollow logs and stumps, thickets, and even going in muskrat dens in search of food. The mink is an excellent fisher, his agility being such as to enable him to catch trout and other swiftly swimming fishes with ease. He is an active animal, both in summer and in winter, but sometimes "holes up" during extreme cold spells in late winter. His fur primes fairly early in the winter, and often becomes paler and thinner toward late winter and early spring. The best mink skins are usually taken from animals captured in midwinter, when the fur is dark and glossy.

In most sections, mink bring forth their young in April and May. These are usually born in a nest in an old abandoned muskrat den, or in a crevice beneath a rock. Sometimes mink have their young in a hollow log or stump, or beneath a big dry drift. Nearly always the location will be near water—on the bank of a stream or lake, or at the edge of a swamp, bayou, or bit of marsh. The mother mink hides the young, as the male will often kill and eat his offspring. The young grow rapidly, and by early fall are able to fend for themselves.

The so-called cotton mink is a sort of freak, rather than a distinct species. It is more commonly found in the Southern, Southwestern, and Central sections. This mink in no way differs from other mink, except in its fur, which is of a white, cottony nature next to the skin. Many a lad has caught one of these mink, fully expecting to sell the skin at a good price, only to be rudely awakened to his error when the fur-buyer pointed out to him the small value of such fur. Cotton mink can readily be recognized by blowing into the fur. White fur next to the skin tells the tale.

The weasel makes a track very similar to that of the mink; but the weasel track is much smaller, and usually shows the claw-marks more distinctly. Although the weasel uses about many of the same places that are frequented by mink, it almost never wades in the water. Close observation will readily enable anyone to distinguish mink tracks and signs wherever found.

Look for mink droppings on logs and about drifts. They are slightly larger than those of the muskrat, much darker, and some-times contain fur or hair. Often, too, one will find where a mink has killed a bird or a rabbit. And look closely for the tracks of this animal in paths in thickets, or at the edges of streams or ponds. Quite often one will see tracks and signs among the ex-posed roots of trees along creek banks. Too, you are almost certain to find signs of this animal about old muskrat dens or in many of the paths and runways in marshes or swamps. Investigate all out-of-the-way places near water, for these are the spots where mink most frequently are found.

Best Methods of Trapping the Mink

Although many trappers have good success in using den sets and bait sets in trapping the mink, perhaps most trappers will find the trail set and the blind set better for trapping this animal. Find where the animals have been passing through an opening in a drift, or where they have been using a runway through a hollow log, and set a No. 1 or No. 1½ trap here, covering it carefully with material that will fit in well with the surroundings. This is one of the best sets I have ever used for taking the mink. Or go along a stream or pond where there are mink tracks until you come to a place where the animals are forced to travel in shallow water to get around a tree, bush, rock, or other natural object on the bank. Set your trap in about two inches of water at this place, being careful to get it positioned so that it will be within the line of travel and to see that it is well covered with water-soaked leaves, moss, or other natural covering material. Sometimes the tracks at such a place show that the animals have been traveling over a rather wide area. Then it is well to narrow down the area of travel by placing a stone out a little way in the water or by using a stick or a brush to confine the travel to a narrow area near the edge of the water. I frequently use this set in early winter, before heavy freezing causes the forming of shore ice. It is a most excellent set for fall and early winter trapping.

Traps may be set on logs, where there are mink droppings to show that they are being used by the animals; or they may be set at root wads, or in runways in thickets. Occasionally one will find

Arched Root Set. Trap Beneath the Water. Drowning Stake in Use.

where mink have been traveling beneath an arched root or around the corner of a bridge abutment. Such places make excellent set locations. Old muskrat dens that are not being used by the 'rats are very good places for trapping for mink, as are also trails through flag beds and runways beneath overhanging banks. Overflow branches from springs are good places for sets, especially in winter, when severe freezing has locked most streams and ponds in ice. Look for sheltered places for your traps when deep snows come, such as beneath overhanging banks, under big drifts, beneath evergreen trees, and in hollow logs. Tile outlets in sheltered places often provide good set locations at such times.

Mink are frequently trapped at dens—their own, as well as the old unused ones of other animals. During cold weather, mink sometimes do a great deal of traveling, at which times they visit dens wherever they find them. At such times, a trap set at any old den anywhere along a stream or lake shore is likely to catch mink. When snows come, one can often locate the animal's den by following the tracks to it. When the den has several openings, each should be trapped, or else all but one should be securely blocked. To my way of thinking, though, den trapping—at the animal's own den—is a rather poor method of taking mink, since a catch will often frighten away other mink using the same den or other dens in that vicinity. It is a much better plan to set traps in trails at some little distance from the den than to place the trap at the den or within the den opening. This reasoning will also apply to hollow trees or hollow logs when used as dens by this animal, but not to such places when merely used as frequenting spots or runways.

Mossy logs bridging small streams are good places to set traps for mink. However, look well to the fastenings of your traps at such sets, for you may take other fur-bearers at these places, such as the fox or the raccoon. If you know of a beaver dam on some wild mountain stream, don't fail to examine it closely for mink signs. Make your sets in the shallow places when at all possible, and use the drowning wire fastening. Log heaps and brush heaps along streams are good places for mink traps. And don't fail to leave traps at holes beneath haystacks, for mink use such places when hunting for rabbits and mice.

When using baits in mink trapping, some trappers build artificial bait pens, bait cubbies, or bait holes, while others place the baits at natural locations. The latter method is to be preferred when suitable set locations can be found.

Artificial bait pens may be made of pieces of bark, slabs of rock, chunks of wood, and the like. Some use short sticks, making the pen in the form of a circle and leaving an opening at that point where the animal is most likely to approach the bait. Old weathered sticks are better for this purpose than freshly cut sticks or sticks that have been barked. Such a bait pen will be more effective if it is partly hidden by brush or leaves. All bait pens should be covered with bark or some such material, so as to protect the baits from the sharp vision of crows, buzzards, and owls.

An artificial bait hole of considerable worth is made by digging a hole at a suitable location in the bank of a stream, with the bait—part of a rabbit, muskrat, or fish—placed at the back end and the trap set in a couple of inches of water at the opening. Artificial lures or natural animal scents may be used in connection with this set. The hole, which should be about five or six inches in diameter, need not be more than twelve inches deep. All dirt removed in digging it should be thrown far out into deep water. Make a few imitation claw-marks about the opening. These will tend to improve your chances of making a catch.

In my opinion, natural bait sets are to be preferred wherever they can be used to advantage. Good locations for these are at crevices beneath shelving rock, at hollows at the bases of trees and stumps, or in natural recesses in drifts. A very effective set of this kind may be made around root wads, at the end of hollow logs, or in small washed-out places in stream banks. I like to use natural baits at such places, although artificial baits or natural scents may often produce good results. An improvement may be added by scattering a few bird feathers about the set.

Among the natural baits used for trapping the mink, none is better than rabbit or muskrat. Small birds—pests, such as sparrows, crows, starlings, and the like—are excellent baits, too. Fish make good baits when placed where they will appear as if they had been accidentally dropped or discarded by roving animals. In placing any bait, it is a good plan to cover it partly with dead leaves, dry grass, or trash, so as to make it appear as if it might be the hidden remnant of the former meal of some animal.

Use baits rather sparingly. And do not have too many in any given locality. Better success will result from the use of a few good bait sets scattered over a wide area than when several are crowded into a rather restricted area.

Valuing Mink Skins

In skinning mink, leave the claws on the pelt and remove all the bone from the tail. Split the skin half way or more to the tip of the tail, then slip it off the bone the remainder of the way by use of the thumb and forefinger, or by making use of a small split stick. It is a good plan to slit the skin all the way to the tip of the tail after it has been slipped off the bone; otherwise spoilage here in warm weather may damage the pelt. Skin the animal so as to have a cased pelt. Work carefully around the ears, eyes, nose, and mouth, so as not to cut or otherwise damage the skin. Stretch the hide as long as possible, but do not overstretch. Dimensions for mink stretchers and directions for skinning animals have been given elsewhere in this book.

Mink skins are valued according to size, color, and primeness.

Prime skins with dark fur bring the most money. A skin is prime when the fur—not the guard hairs—is silky and long, and the flesh side shows an even pinkish color throughout. Dull, leatherish color —in streaks, patches, or over the entire flesh side of the pelt—indicates an unprime or partly prime skin.

Mink Tracks in Snow—Animal Running.

Chapter XVI

Trapping the Skunk

Skunks are found in practically all parts of the United States and northward well into Canada. They appear in greatest numbers in farming communities and ranching countries, although they often are found in less numbers in mountainous and semiwilderness sections. There are several species. In Southern sections, the animals are usually small, rarely exceeding seven pounds in weight; but in more Northern sections they grow to greater size, often attaining a weight of ten to twelve or more pounds.

The skunk is twenty-seven to thirty-six inches long, measuring from the tip of the nose to the tip of the tail. The fur is dense, with a generous covering of long guard hairs. The tail is usually twelve to fifteen inches long. It is covered with long hair, the color of which varies with the general color of the fur on the body of the animal. Thus, a black skunk or one with but little white on the body commonly has a black tail, with or without a white tip; while a skunk that has lots of white in the fur on its body will usually have a black and white tail, or maybe a tail that is mostly white.

Skunks are classified by raw fur dealers according to the amount of white fur that appears on the body. The "star" or black skunk usually is entirely black, except for a short, white pencil line between the eyes and sometimes a white tail tip. A variation of this sort is the skunk with a roundish white spot on top of the head with two fingers of white reaching an inch or so back on the short, thick neck. Such skunks are known as "baldies." The short-stripe skunk is marked exactly like a "baldy," except that the fingers of white are usually a little broader and reach back in a narrow "V" to a point just beyond the middle of the back. The long-stripe or narrow-stripe skunk has these white stripes reaching the entire length of the body. The space between these stripes widens at the center of the back and narrows again near the tail. The stripes are frequently wider near the center of the body. The tail is covered with an intermixture of black and white hairs. And the broad-stripe skunk has much wider stripes of white. These vary in width in different animals, some having almost no black fur on them. The tail of this skunk is white, or nearly white.

There is a one-striped skunk appearing in Southwestern sections. It has a single broad white stripe running from the forehead down the back to the root of the tail. There is also a little spotted skunk in Texas and other Southwestern parts of the country. It is known as the polecat or civit cat. The hognosed skunk appears in a rather restricted area in southern Arizona, but is of little importance to trappers in general, since it occurs so far south and has so much white on it that its fur is of little value.

Skunks are night-roving animals, but are occasionally seen wandering around in the daytime. They frequent thickets, brier patches, neglected pastures, and love to use about old, tumble-down farm buildings and brier-grown fence rows. The animal's diet is widely varied, quite commonly consisting of such items as grubs and worms, bugs, grasshoppers, snakes, frogs, mice, and birds. Skunks will often eat roots and berries, too; and they devour great numbers of the eggs of ground-nesting birds. Occasionally a skunk will visit a farm poultry house to vary its diet with chicken meat or eggs.

Once a year, usually in April or May, the skunk brings forth a litter of six to nine young. The animal cares for its young throughout the summer until such time as the little ones are able to care for themselves, which is usually not until extremely late summer or early fall. The young are born in a nest of dry leaves or grass, either in a den or hollow log, or at well-hidden places beneath old farm buildings, haystacks or strawstacks, or log heaps. After the young attain some little growth, the mother skunk begins to take them out with her on foraging trips. It is no uncommon sight in late summer to see a mother skunk out in the daytime with her young following her like a litter of pigs tagging along after a sow.

WHERE SKUNKS ARE FOUND

Skunks use about old brier-grown pastures, neglected fence rows, and briery thickets, where their dens may often be found. Occasionally one will find groups of skunk dens in rather open country, often on steep hillsides, usually in brier patches or among clumps of small bushes. Again, one may see them at the edges of woods, or perhaps less frequently far back in the woods where there is much undergrowth. Not infrequently one will see the small holes in the ground in woods and pastures where the animals have been digging for grubs and worms. Quite often one will find places in thickets and along brier-grown fence rows where they have killed and eaten small birds and mice. Like the fox, they often dig around old rotting stumps for food. One will not infrequently see their tracks in the dust in paths and runways after a spell of dry weather; and in early winter it is no uncommon sight after a snowfall to observe their trails crossing and recrossing everywhere in the thickets and woods.

Rocky hillsides are good places to look for skunk dens. Being a somewhat sluggish and rather lazy animal, the skunk frequently occupies the old dens of other animals rather than going to the trouble of digging its own dens. It generally does not travel great distances, commonly remaining throughout life in or near the locality where it was born. So if one knows where there are old dens in skunk country, one is fairly certain to find at least some of them occupied by this animal, especially if they are well hidden among briers and clumps of elder. Examine the openings to such dens for long black and white hairs, which may often be found in the dirt there. Sometimes they may be found sticking to protruding roots or clinging to the walls of the den. If a den has been occupied by skunks for any great length of time, there are likely to be droppings of the animal at one or more places near by. These droppings will often be found grouped rather than scattered about, and will nearly always show pieces of bugs, tiny wisps of bird down, or bits of the fur of mice.

The trail of the skunk somewhat resembles one made by a house cat, only the tracks are not so round, the claw-marks are more conspicuous, and the footprints are much closer together. Skunk trails show that the animals wander around in an aimless manner a great deal, zigzagging about among the sprouts and briers, often covering a route of several rods to reach a point only a few feet away. The animal's aimless wandering reminds one of the irregular ramblings of a lost lamb or pig. Sometimes, however, skunks travel with more directness, covering considerable distance. This commonly happens in the spring, when the animals are frequently thin and their food supply is scarce. I have known them to travel several miles in a single night at such times, not infrequently visiting every den along their route of travel.

METHODS OF TRAPPING

Without doubt, more skunks are taken in steel traps than by any other method, although many of them lose their lives in an unequal race with a night-hunting dog. Years ago, the deadfall was widely used in trapping this animal; but the advent of the steel trap caused trappers to modernize their methods of skunk trapping. Perhaps no other animal is so frequently captured at den sets and bait sets. Thousands are caught yearly by inexperienced trappers, many of whom set their traps only at the openings of dens. Formerly, before the method was prohibited by law in many parts of the country, great numbers of skunks were captured by digging them out of their dens with spade and pick. This, of course, is a wasteful practice, and one that should be made illegal in all sections. For it should be clear that when the dens are destroyed in any locality, the skunks must move out to other places. Experienced trappers usually trap for this animal with trail sets, blind sets, and bait sets, perhaps using a few den sets at favorable selected locations.

Most professional trappers use the No. 1 trap—or traps of corresponding size—for catching the skunk. In certain sections in the Northwestern and North-central parts of the country, where this animal grows to a very large size, it perhaps would be advisable to use larger traps, say, the No. 1½ or corresponding size. Skunks are often bad actors in traps. They are commonly docile, seldom flouncing around or exerting themselves greatly to escape from the trap. But they have the bad habit of gnawing off a foot just below the trap jaws. Some trappers endeavor to prevent such happenings by using traps with specially made jaws. Others prevent the happening largely by using a light drag or clog when fastening traps.

The trapper who hopes to make a good catch of skunks will make several trips early in the fall to the locality where he expects to do his trapping, spending on each trip as much time as possible in looking up skunk dens and locating the trails where the animals are in the habit of using. Then he will know not only where the animals are denning, but where to find the best places to set his traps. He will know where the best locations for trail sets may be found, and where he can find the best natural locations for bait sets.

Wherever there are a number of skunk dens in a group, one will nearly always find many worn trails leading away in several directions. Such trails will often furnish one with several good places for making sets; for each trail may well be guarded with two or more traps set at some little distance from the dens. However, it is a good plan to set only one trap, or maybe none, in any short trail that fades out quickly near the den. At such places, do your trapping as far as possible away from the dens. Unused stock paths in old pastures make good places for using trail sets, as also do furrows, dry gullies, or small dry ditches where the animals have been using. Look closely in thickets for skunk droppings or other skunk signs, especially along trails or near dens. Many times one will thus be able to determine definitely that skunks are using thereabouts. One can then go ahead and make trail sets and blind sets with quite some likelihood of making catches.

Blind sets may sometimes be used with good results in trapping for skunks. A trapper will often catch this animal in traps set at openings in dry drifts; at holes beneath fences; around the bases of culverts over dry ditches; at paths or runways around haystacks, log heaps, or near dens at dams or in dry stream banks; and in paths near fruiting persimmon trees. Before setting traps at any such locations, be sure that skunk are using in the vicinity.

Next to the trail set, perhaps the bait set is more used by professional trappers than any other for taking the skunk. The bait generally consists of chicken, rabbit, birds, or the carcass of the skunk itself. Dead livestock of any kind will serve well for bait, for the skunk relishes putrid meat as well as, or better than, meat that is fresh. One caution, however, should be mentioned in connection with this sort of trapping; try to set your traps in such locations that they will not be likely to catch farm dogs.

Many skunk dens in early fall will show scratched places about the entrances, where skunks have been raking in dry grass or dead leaves to build winter beds. Not all skunk dens will show such signs, however, for many times the animals will carry in material for bed-making without leaving signs. Some skunk dens will show balled dirt at the entrances, something like that found at woodchuck dens. But many dens will show merely as slanting holes

Hollow Log Set. A good one for trapping skunks, opossums, raccoons, foxes, and minks. Baits may be used in making this set.

beneath rocks or logs, at stumps or the bases of trees, without fresh dirt at the entrances, which frequently may be rimmed with dead vegetation.

When setting a trap at a den, one should see that it is placed a little to one side of the central part of the opening and not too far within the throat of the den. As a rule, skunk spread their feet a little as they enter or leave a den, and therefore are more likely to place a foot in a trap that is located a little to one side of the center of the den floor. Too, when an animal enters or leaves a den, its belly drags on this part of the den floor. A trap centrally located is therefore more apt to catch a wisp of belly fur or hair than it is to close on a foot or leg.

Always scoop out a shallow depression for the trap, lining it carefully with dry dead leaves, dry grass, moss, or the like; and be sure that the trap is covered with the same material as that which was removed in making the set. At dens, this is often dry dirt or sand. No matter—use it for covering material. Fit. a piece of very thin paper or a thin dead leaf between the trap jaws so as to fill completely this space; or cover the entire trap very lightly with crumpled dry leaves or coarsely powdered dry grass. Then sprinkle powdered dirt or dry sand lightly over the entire set. Use the dirt or sand sparingly. Too much will clog the trap when an animal springs it.

Don't use too many den sets at any given location. I remember I was guilty of this practice when I first began to trap, and I always was wondering why I could not catch many skunk at a colony of dens. I did not know I was frightening the animals away by using too many sets. As a rule, skunks are not easily disturbed by trapping; but too many den sets at a place will sometimes cause the animals to move out to a new locality. If you plan to set many traps in a rather restricted area, place most of them in trails or at blind set locations at some little distance from the dens. By thus placing your traps, you may not catch quite so many animals the first few nights, but you will have better trapping over a longer period.

Several methods of killing captured skunks have been advocated by various writers and trappers. Some drown the catch; others paralyze the animal by striking it a sharp blow across the back with a club to keep it from throwing its scent, then killing it; still others approach the trapped animal very slowly and strike it a quick blow at the base of the skull. I have tried them all—often to my sorrow. The best way I have found to kill a captured skunk is to shoot it in the center of the forehead, just above the level of the eyes, at a distance of twelve to fifteen feet with a good 22 cal. rifle or pistol.

USING BAITS

Baits play such a big part in skunk trapping in many sections that it has been thought advisable to write a bit about the use of them. Some trappers pin their faith largely to the use of artificial baits and scents in trapping this animal. Others hold to the view that natural baits are best. However, the decision here rests entirely with the individual trapper. It is a good plan to try both methods; then one can hold to the method that gives the better results. Personally, the use of natural baits has always been quite satisfactory in my trapping.

Among the fresh baits that I have used in trapping this animal are such items as domestic fowls, birds, rabbits, skunk carcasses, hen's eggs, muskrat flesh, and bloody pieces of refuse meat from butcher houses. One trapping in semiwilderness sections would likely use such baits as birds, rabbits, and the carcasses of trapped animals. Stale and putrid baits are often better attractors than fresh baits. Dead chickens, ducks, or turkeys make fine baits of this kind, as do also the carcasses of livestock. Some trappers drag a piece of putrid meat through the woods and thickets, then set traps at suitable places along the line of travel, either with or without baits. But I have never found this plan to be noticeably effective.

To be of greatest worth, baits should be half-hidden in thickets and woods at such locations that appear to be most natural and therefore most likely to be visited by wandering animals. Pin down the carcass of a chicken or a duck at a point where two or more trails cross in a thicket; or fasten a dead rabbit back under the end of a log that protrudes over a vine-covered depression in the woods; or stake a piece of putrid meat among sprouts where clumps of them stand near a creek bank; or fasten a dead bird—crow, starling, or sparrow—back under the ends of overhanging logs at the end of a log heap. But first be sure that skunks are using in the vicinity. It will help, too, to cover a part of each bait with dry leaves, dead grass, or something that fits in well with the surroundings. Don't forget to set traps around the carcasses of any farm animals that you find on your trap line, keeping in mind the necessity of making such sets as will be least likely to take farm dogs. Above all, don't forget that a stale skunk carcass makes a skunk bait second to none!

Grading and Valuing Skunk Skins

Skunk skins are graded and valued according to size, color, and primeness. The skunk does not grow heavy fur nor take on the fat between the skin and body that makes for primeness in the pelt until after a reasonably long period of cold weather; so its skin often does not become fully prime until late in the fall. A fully prime skin is full-furred, has glossy fur, and shows a flesh side that is white with a pinkish tinge where muscular tissue appears on the pelt. The fatty tissue is nearly white, not yellowish; and the pelt is substantially thick and heavy.

The No. 1 or black skunk skin is the most valuable. The No. 2 or short-stripe skin grades next in value; while the No. 3 or long-stripe skin and the No. 4 or broad-stripe skin are graded downward in value respectively. All skunk skins are graded as to size—large, medium, and small. If fur skins have been properly handled, dealers will sometimes "stretch a point" in size grading, allowing the same price for medium skins as is quoted for large skins and the same price for small skins as is quoted for medium skins. It pays in more ways than one always to do the skinning, stretching, fleshing, and curing jobs with utmost care.

Skunk Tracks—Animal Walking.

Chapter XVII

How to Trap the Raccoon

Being nocturnal in its habits, the raccoon is seldom seen in the daytime. It is an excellent swimmer and a good climber. When chased by night-hunting dogs, it will put up a good chase. If closely pursued, it will often show considerable craftiness in its efforts to evade its pursuers. It can climb trees nimbly, and not infrequently jumps surprising distances from one tree to another or from the limb of a tree to the ground, always alighting in catlike fashion on its feet and racing away to lead its tormentors in another lively chase.

The raccoon is found in nearly all parts of North America from Florida to the Hudson Bay and from Texas to Vancouver Island. It is more plentiful in Southern sections, however, but does not grow so large here. Its fur is most valuable in such Northern parts of the country as Minnesota, Wisconsin, Michigan, and the Northeastern states from Pennsylvania to Maine. A full-grown animal will weigh twenty-five to forty pounds, being from twenty-eight to thirty-six inches in length, measuring from the tip of the nose to the tip of the tail. The tail, which is five to eight inches long, is ringed its full length with alternating bands of equal width of brownish and blackish fur.

Raccoons are most commonly found in swamps, marshes, and wooded lowlands. They love to wander along wooded streams and about lake shores, where they find frogs, crayfish, and small fish. They eat insects, birds' eggs, frogs, fish, mussels, birds, corn, and such fruits as persimmons, wild grapes, and many kinds of wild berries. When in the vicinity of water, the raccoon will nearly always wash its food before eating it. When fighting in self-defense, this animal is a vicious fighter; but it will very seldom attack other animals when unprovoked. It has been known to whip three or four dogs when cornered and fighting for its life. It fights much like a common house cat, using both claws and teeth, often while lying on its back. In Northern sections, this animal commonly hibernates or sleeps for as long as a couple or three months, usually during cold spells. In most Southern parts, it is active throughout the year.

Haunts and Habits of the Raccoon

Wherever raccoons are found, there will be woods and waters not far away. For this animal loves to wander about wooded lake shores, streams, and timbered swamps and marshes, where frogs, small fish, and wild fruits may be had in plenty. It lives in hollow trees. Sometimes it dens in the ground, usually beneath rock ledges, but occasionally in ground dens in or near a woods.

Rippling, rock-bedded streams and the wooded shores of lakes and bayous are favorite haunts of this animal. It loves to wade in rocky shallows, where it often spends much time on moonlit nights searching for mussels, crayfish, frogs, and other water creatures. Corn fields that are bordered by woods are favorite spots for the raccoon, especially in late summer, when the ears of corn are in the milky stage. But the animal likes mature corn, too, and is frequently found around corn cribs and about corn fields even during the winter. It also prowls about a great deal in dense thickets and along spring-fed brooks at the edges of grassy swamps and marshes. Hilly sections that are covered with timber are usually inhabited by raccoons, especially if small brooks and half-hidden springs are common to the area.

The tracks of this animal are sprawling, especially when seen in mud or snow. Those of the forefeet are spreading, showing the full imprint of the long, slim toes; while those of the hind feet are long and somewhat resemble in form the tracks made by a tiny child. When loping, the raccoon places two feet close together, but when walking, it keeps its feet farther apart. The trail of the animal is distinctive and almost unmistakable. However, inexperienced trappers do sometimes mistake the trails of woodchucks for those of raccoons. But it will be noticed that the imprint of the heel of the woodchuck is much shorter than that of the heel of the raccoon and is not nearly so distinct. Too, the trails will show that the woodchuck places all four feet close together, while the raccoon keeps its feet a little farther apart.

Raccoons love to run on frosty moonlit nights in the fall. These are the sort of nights one will find them at the edges of woods near swampy ground or far back in the deep woods. Log-strewn thickets are frequent haunts of this animal on such nights. They love to run on misty, damp, warm nights, too. These are the sort of nights when 'coon hunters will take to the woods with their night-hunting dogs. During extremely cold spells in midwinter, the raccoon commonly "holes up" in some den or hollow in a tree, coming out to feed only when the weather moderates. Raccoons frequently travel about a great deal, sometimes covering several miles in a single night. Often a trapper can find their den trees by following their tracks in soft snow. Rarely there are as many as half a dozen raccoons in a single den tree; but commonly only one or, at most, two will be found.

Trapping Methods Used

Most trappers use the trail set or the blind set for taking the raccoon, although some trap it at its den in rocky cliffs or in the ground. Trapping at den trees is unlawful in some parts of the country, but formerly many were captured in this way. The practice is still followed in those sections where the local laws do not prevent such trapping. In early days, many raccoons were captured by cutting the den trees; but, owing to the increasing value of timber and the growing scarcity of raccoons, this wasteful practice is fast being discontinued in practically all parts of the country.

The raccoon is not difficult to trap, except when it has been nipped a few times by poorly set traps. Then it frequently gets to be almost as crafty as the fox, and is no less difficult to trap. This animal has the weakness of stopping to investigate most any shining object in the water. When wading the riffles of streams or roaming along the shores of bayous or ponds in search of food, it will stop to paw over any shining piece of mussel shell, bright rock, or other bright object, apparently out of pure curiosity. This peculiar habit has cost many a raccoon its life. For trappers have learned that a trap set in shallow, swift water near the bank of a stream with some bright object—such as a piece of tinfoil or bright tin—attached to the pan will take the animal fairly regularly, especially on moonlit nights. However, such traps should always be covered, except the pan with its shining lure.

Trappers do not all agree on the right size of trap for this animal. Some use the No. 1½ trap, claiming it is sufficiently strong to hold this animal when a light clog fastening is used. Others claim that nothing smaller than a No. 2 trap should ever be used for trapping it. I think no little of this diversity of opinion is caused by the difference in the size of this animal in various parts of the country. In Midwestern and certain Southern sections, some few trappers use the No. 1 trap. In my opinion this trap is a little too light for such use. I think the No. 1½ trap is the one to choose for use in most parts of the country. Fastened to a movable drag or clog, this trap, I believe, will be found to give entire satisfaction.

When making trail sets or blind sets for raccoons, one will do well to look for set locations near or at the edge of the water. Find where the animals have been passing between a stone or other object on the bank and the edge of the pond or stream. Or look for narrow passageways in drifts or around bushes, stumps, or logs at the edge of the water. A log lying with one end on the bank and the other end in the water makes a fine location for a set. Place the trap in a niche chopped out of the top of the log at a point just below the surface of the water; or the trap may be set on land at the place where the animal climbs up on the log; or a set may be made at each location. Many raccoons are caught in traps that have been set at the ends of logs bridging small streams. One should make such sets very carefully, however, since traps set at such locations are likely to catch other animals, such as fox, mink, or otter. Many raccoons are taken in traps set on the tops of muskrat houses. Unused stock paths or deer trails near a stream or swamp are good places for trapping this animal. Traps set for raccoons should always be well hidden. Light clogs or drowning wires should be used in fastening the traps. Where neither is practical, use a long wire fastening.

Many trappers like to take the raccoon at bait sets. Flesh baits are commonly used at such sets. Fish, chicken, birds, bloody muskrat flesh—all are good for bait. Any of these baits make excellent lures when half-hidden near trails or runways beside streams or near swamps. Be careful to place them so that an animal will have to step on the pan of the trap to reach them. Some trappers use fish heads in bait cubbies. However, this bait will make a better lure if it is used at natural locations. Heavily fruited persimmon trees make excellent locations for sets. Find where the animals have been traveling between some object and the base of the tree, or where they have been climbing the tree. Traps set at such locations will usually take them.

Artificial lures are used by many trappers for taking the raccoon. Anise oil is much used, as are many of the various commercial lures containing fish oil. Some of these may be used to advantage as attractors, but many of them are better for attracting money to their makers than for attracting raccoons to sets. Usually one will find that natural sets and natural baits will be all that is needed. In my experience, I have never felt the need of using artificial lures in trapping this animal.

Den Trees and Den Locations

It is commonly assumed that the raccoon lives in holes in trees. This is not always the case. Often it dens among the rocks, or in a hole beneath a rock ledge, or in well-hidden dens almost any place in the ground. I have known them to den in hollow logs and stumps. But perhaps more raccoons den in holes in trees than in other locations, particularly in those sections where timber is fairly plentiful.

One can often locate den trees by tracking the raccoon to them during thaws or at times when there is a soft snow on the ground. Quite frequently the den tree will be a big oak, sycamore, maple, or hickory. Seldom does the animal select small hollow trees for den sites. Yet I have seen them den in old hollow snags. I have always had better success in trapping the animal in trails near a den tree than I had when trapping them at the tree itself. Usually several faint trails will be noticeable leading to the base of a den tree. Here is where I place my traps—back some little distance from the base of the tree. If a log lies near the den tree, a trap set in a notch chopped in it and carefully covered will be a very good set. A raccoon will always approach a leaning den tree from the high side. He will nearly always jump up on the trunk when within some twenty to thirty inches of the tree. Likewise, when leaving the tree, the animal will usually jump off when it gets within a foot or so of the ground.

Ground dens or dens beneath rock ledges are often well hidden, not infrequently being behind bushes or beneath brush heaps. Often inaccessible dens far back in crevices in rock cliffs or beneath rock ledges can only be located by such tracks and signs as may appear at or near the entrance to the crevices or fissures. Dense thickets with many logs and much debris in evidence are good places to look for ground dens. When trapping in such places, it is much better to place the traps in trails and runways near the dens that to place them at the den openings. However, if traps *are* set at the den openings, be sure to see that they are placed in shallow depressions and carefully covered. And have them a little to one side of the center of the den entrance.

Judging the Value of Raccoon Skins

Raccoons are commonly skinned so as to produce an open pelt. This is accomplished by slitting the skin down the underside of the animal's body from the chin to the vent, then across the body at the hindlegs and the forelegs from one foot to the other. Full directions for skinning so as to produce an open skin are given elsewhere in this book. All tags and uneven points of the skin should be cut away, so as to have the skin comparatively square when the stretching job is finished. It will sometimes be found necessary to stretch certain parts of the skin more than other parts, in order to make a perfectly square pelt.

Raccoon skins are graded both as to size and color. Primeness, of course, is always a consideration. Dark-furred skins from the Northern sections are most valuable. Some of the finest raccoon skins come from the northern tier of states in the United States and from central and eastern sections of Canada. To be fully prime, a raccoon skin should have heavy, even fur, with the flesh side showing fairly white or a little pinkish. A bluish or brownish tinge on the flesh side indicates a skin not fully prime.

Raccoon Tracks—Animal Walking.

Chapter XVIII

Fox Trapping

Foxes are found in practically all parts of the world. There are many species, not a few of which are indigenous to the United States and Canada. Perhaps the two best known are the red fox and the gray fox, both of which are found in the United States. The gray fox inhabits the Southern, Eastern, and Northeastern parts, while the red fox is fairly common throughout the Northern three-fourths of the country and over much of Canada. Several color variations of the red fox, which are known by various names, appear in many Northern sections, from the northern part of the United States northward to the Arctic Circle.

In form, the fox greatly resembles the domestic dog. It exists in several predominating colors—black, red, gray, white, blue, silver-gray, and mixed colors. When full grown, the red fox will measure around thirty-eight to forty-four inches from the tip of the nose to the tip of the tail. Its weight is from thirty to thirty-five pounds. The gray fox is somewhat smaller. Both species are found in farming communities as well as in wilderness sections, although the gray fox is usually found in greater numbers in those parts of the country where there is timber.

These animals are very fleet of foot, and often use no little strategy in hunting birds and small animals for food. Being tireless runners, they not infrequently lead pursuing hounds a long, hard, chase. Although the animals are nocturnal in their habits, they sometimes may be seen out wandering about in weed fields, thickets, or deep woods during the daylight hours. One may sometimes see them in the dusk of early morning, slowly walking down some old stock path in a back pasture; or maybe one will meet with them in the dusk of evening, trotting sedately along at the edge of a dense woods.

Foxes mate very early in the spring. They commonly have but one litter a year. From four to nine puppies are born to the litter —usually in a leafy or grassy nest in a den in the ground or beneath a rock ledge, but sometimes in a crevise in the rock or in a hollow log. I have known them to have their young beneath haystacks and brush heaps, as well as beneath old farm buildings. Usually in about five or six weeks the young will come out of the nesting place to play and frolic in the sun. As they grow older, they become more active, often straying several yards from the den or nest. At this age, the mother takes them out on short hunting trips, teaching them how to prey on live birds and animals. Usually the young stay in the nest until they are five or six months old.

The natural enemies of the fox are the wolf, lynx, and fisher. Occasionally one will be killed by an eagle. But by far the greater number of foxes lose their lives in steel traps, although some few are killed by night hunters and fox chasers. However, most fox chasers will seldom kill one of these animals, as they commonly hunt for the sport of the chase only.

HABITS—WHERE TO FIND FOXES

No other fur-bearer in America is quite so difficult to trap as a fox that has become "trap wise" because of having had its toes pinched in steel traps. Such a fox seems to take great delight in foiling the trapper at every turn. He seems to enjoy bringing out all the natural cunning he possesses. And, believe me, he certainly is not at all short on this commodity! It is often stated by uninformed persons that foxes in wilderness sections are less difficult to trap than those found in the vicinity of farms and ranches. However, the opposite is much nearer the truth. Foxes inhabiting farming communities are more accustomed to the scent of man and more used to seeing changes in their surroundings. They are therefore often less suspicious of strange scents and unusual changes than are the foxes in the backwoods sections. However, a "trap wise" fox is something else, regardless of whether it is in a farming community or in wilderness territory.

Foxes are great hunters. They use both eyesight and sense of smell in locating their natural food, which is rabbits, mice, birds, and the like. When possible, they take advantage of the wind in their hunting, always keeping their stealthy movements well screened by bushes or clumps of grass as they approach their victims from the down-wind side. They are excellent jumpers, not infrequently pouncing upon a bird or a rabbit from a distance of several feet, clearing any low obstruction that may be between them and their prospective meal. They love to hunt rabbits on moonlit nights, when they search them out in tall grass or weeds, and frequently surprise them at play at the edges of woods. They dig for mice and shrews about old rotting stumps and logs, and catch many small birds in brier patches and thickets. They often follow fresh furrows in order to pick up the shrews and mice that are found there. Rather rarely, they visit the farmer's or rancher's poultry house and carry off a nice fat hen for their young.

Wooded areas and rocky hillsides in the vicinity of extended rock ledges are good places to look for fox signs. Such areas are all the better if there happens to be several hillside springs and swift, crooked, bush-choked branches in the locality. Foxes use much on high sand ridges, too. Old pastures and meadows are nearly always frequented by foxes, as are many of the old haystacks and straw-stacks, where the animals go to search for mice. Foxes sometimes use in wooded lowlands along rivers, or near marshes or swamps. But sand ridges bordering on marshes or swamps seem to have special attraction for this animal.

When searching for fox tracks and signs, one should examine all such places as stock trails in old pastures, old unused tote-roads, clearings, animal trails in thickets, rock cliffs, briery fence rows, springs, log crossings at small streams, openings beneath fences, culverts, and the like. Sometimes one will not see tracks; but there may be claw-marks, or maybe a hair or two will be found clinging to a splinter on a fence rail or a picket; or perhaps there will be droppings. Always look for places where the animal has made a kill. It is a certainty that it will return to the spot when it again passes that way. It is wise to keep alert to all such possibilities when out looking for fox signs. Foxes often have certain places where they go through openings in fences, cross streams, or travel stock paths. Find these, and your chances of trapping a fox are good, provided you are careful in making the set.

TRAPPING METHODS IN USE

There are almost as many methods of trapping the fox as there are fox trappers. Some pin their faith to the dirt-hole set; others swear by the water-hole set; still others believe in the chaff-bed set; not a few use sets in connection with artificial or natural scents; and there are those who trap the animal in trail sets and blind sets, much as they would trap the mink. Since there are so many methods used in trapping this animal, I shall mention only a few of the more successful ones that I have tried and found good. The reader will do well to try all the methods he can contrive, then stick to those that are most successful.

Ant Hill Set for Foxes.

A very successful set that I have used is the ant-hill set. These ant hills are small conical-shaped mounds of dirt thrown up by colonies of ants. You will find them in the woods and fields, usually on hilly or ridge land. Sometimes they are as large as a small haycock, being three feet high and four feet across at the base; but usually they are much smaller—a foot high and eighteen inches across. Scoop out a shallow place on top of the mound, line it with dry leaves or dry grass, then place the trap in it and cover over carefully with broad dry leaves or thin paper, after which sprinkle a light layer of dry dirt or sand over the set. Conceal the trap chain by covering it with dirt; and wire it to a clog placed several feet away and hidden beneath dry grass or leaves. You can improve this set wonderfully by using a dried fox foot to make fox tracks over the mound. Foxes use about these ant hills a great deal, which makes them very good locations for sets.

Another good set can be made by throwing down a pile of chaff or wheat straw at some favorable location along a briery fence row or at the edge of a woods and setting a trap at it. The chaff or straw, which should be not too deep, should be in place several weeks in advance of the trapping season, so that the foxes thereabouts will have become accustomed to its presence by the time one wants to set the traps. At the time of putting down the chaff, it is well to conceal a couple of sticks or branches for use in fastening the traps. This makes an excellent set for foxes. It may be greatly improved, however, by baiting—occasionally hiding dead mice or bits of burned cracklings in the chaff. Study the chaff pile carefully in order to determine where to place the traps to best advantage. Fasten the traps to well-hidden drags, which should always be in place at the time the chaff pile is made.

The dirt-hole set is a popular method of taking the fox. It grew out of the habit foxes have of digging small holes in the woods and fields in search of shrews, mice, and moles. Perhaps you have noticed such holes on your rambles about the countryside, or even when on trips far back in semi-wilderness sections. Not infrequently one will see them about old rotting stumps and logs; and again they may be noticed in more open places, often at the edges of woods or in brier patches or thickets in old pastures. They look much like a place where a domestic dog had started to dig out a mouse or a mole. Dirt sets are made to simulate these diggings.

In making these sets, draw out and spread dirt at the entrance, much the same as a fox would do. Do not, however, overdo the spreading job—just enough to have the set look natural. Set the trap in a shallow depression in this fresh dirt, being careful to cover it even, so as not to leave any irregularities in the loose dirt. This is best accomplished by using thin paper or broad, dry leaves to cover the trap, over which is sprinkled a thin layer of well-pulverized dirt or fine sand, depending upon the character of the soil at the set. Be sure to use dry material for covering the set, especially during freezing weather. For best results, place a dead mouse or a dead shrew far back in the hole after the set has been made. However, the set may be used without bait, but usually is somewhat less successful. Traps set at dirt-holes should always be fastened to well-hidden drags.

Trail sets and blind sets are widely used in trapping the fox. My own preference is for these sets. I like to trap the animals in trail sets in old stock paths in pastures. Foxes travel such paths regularly. Little-used roads and footpaths in the woods are good locations for sets, especially in backwoods regions. Old sawmill sites, clearings, and brier-grown slashings are all good places for trapping the animals.

One of the best locations for a fox set is where the animal has been crossing a small stream on a moss-covered log. The trap may be set in a notch cut in the log and covered with shredded moss. Or a thin piece of moss may be cut to fit nicely between the open jaws of the trap on top of the pan, using a very light covering of shredded moss to fill in over the trap jaws. Any trail that foxes use will be good for a trail set. But when making sets on snow, be sure to cover the trap very carefully with powdered snow, brushing out all irregularities with a small evergreen branch.

Rabbits are often something of a nuisance when trapping in thickets or brier patches, especially when making trail sets. They can frequently be foiled, however, by the use of guide sticks placed across the trail near the traps. A rabbit will always jump over such a stick in a flying leap, while a fox will step over it carefully. By setting the trap at the proper distance from the guide stick, one can largely avoid catching unwanted rabbits in such sets. Use rather large guide sticks, and place them about six inches from the traps.

Blind sets can often be made at suitable locations in neglected pastures and along briery fence rows where foxes are known to travel. Plowed furrows, dry ditches and gullies, opening at crevices at rocky bluffs, haystacks and strawstacks, brush heaps in thickets, all are good places for making blind sets. Blind sets may often be made to good advantage near the carcass of some domestic animal, or at some little distance from the offal of deer or bear in sections where big game hunting is practiced. One of the best blind sets I have ever used is made at a suitable location near a fruiting persimmon tree. Foxes love ripe persimmons, and may often be found using about these trees when the ripe fruits begin to fall.

Foxes have the peculiar habit of getting up on a stump, log, or mound to view a bait or other object of interest at a distance. This habit enables trappers to take the fox at bait sets without much risk of catching farm dogs. Place a fresh bait—rabbit or fowl—on a small knoll in the woods where it can be seen from all angles for a distance of several yards. Or one may fasten the bait in the branches of a small bush, or nail it up a few inches on the trunk of a tree or sapling. See that there is a mound or a log somewhere within a dozen feet of the bait. Here is where you want to set the trap, not at the bait. A fox approaching such a bait will circle it, jumping upon whatever he can find to get a better view. If you have been careful to hide your trap well, you will catch him. This is an excellent set to use in any place where farm dogs are likely to get caught in the conventional bait set.

One other very successful fox set might be mentioned—the water-hole set. It is most commonly used at springs, since spring water seldom freezes in ordinary winter weather. You make it by placing a flesh bait on top of a stick some three feet out in a spring or stream, so that the bait seems to be floating on the water. Flat stones are then built up to within two inches of the surface of the water at a point midway between the shore and the bait. Or a single flat-topped stone may be used. The trap is set on this stone. Moss is then worked well around it and over the trap, until the whole appears to be nothing more than a moss-covered stone. This is a most killing set if properly made. Some trappers like to use artificial lure on the bait at this set; but it would appear that the natural bait alone is all that is necessary.

Trapping foxes for bounty is often fairly profitable in those parts where a good bounty is paid for the capture of this animal. Some trappers make this sort of trapping a summer job. Inquiry at the offices of the Department of Conservation of your state or at the county clerk's office in your county will get you information regarding local bounties—amounts paid, what part or parts of the animal to present for bounty, etc. Bounties usually cover all species of any animal. In some parts of the country, the trapper is permitted to sell the skins in addition to getting paid a bounty.

When it comes to trap sizes, we are getting in disputed territory. The No. 1, No. 1½, No. 2, and even the No. 3 trap are used for this animal. However, the No. 1½ and No. 2 traps will be found more nearly suited to the strength of the fox. I have trapped them successfully in No. 1 traps—by using light drag fastenings, but I would recommend heavier traps for best results. There has been a lot of buncombe written about the human scent problem. However, boil your traps well in a cedar or walnut-hull solution and use reasonable care in handling them afterwards, and you will not need to give much further thought to the human scent theory. For that is all it is—theory. One of the best fox trappers I have ever known—my younger brother—always set his fox traps without benefit of gloves or other hand protection. However, the use of leather gloves may sometimes be advisable when trapping for any "trapwise" fox. But don't forget that human scent leaves a trap a few hours after it has been set. And don't forget, either, that a lifetime is not too long to learn all there is to know about trapping the fox.

DETERMINING THE VALUE OF FOX SKINS

Skin foxes so as to produce cased skins. Split the tail and take out the bone. Be careful in skinning about the ears, eyes, nose, and mouth. Leave the feet and claws on the pelt, but skin out all bone. Stretch the skin with the fur side out. There will be no danger of spoilage if care is taken in fleshing, so as to get off all fat and surplus flesh.

The quality of fox fur varies a great deal, even on the skins taken in the same locality. Grading is done largely on the basis of quality, as well as in relation to size. Heavy, silky fur is most wanted, and this sort is usually found on skins taken from foxes from Northern sections. The skins, of course, are classed as large, medium, and small. Primeness, too, is considered, the same as in grading other fur skins. A fox skin is prime when the fur is silky and heavy, and the flesh side of the pelt shows white, with perhaps a pinkish tinge over parts of it. A yellowish or brownish cast on the flesh side of the pelt indicates unprimeness.

Fox Tracks in Snow—Animal Walking.

Chapter XIX

Trapping the Opossum

This grayish, long-haired, pointed-nosed animal with a tail like that of the house rat is native to the eastern half of the United States south of the Great Lakes region. It is found most abundantly in the South and the Southeast. A few are found in southwestern California, where the animal was introduced a few years ago.

The opossum is from twenty-eight to thirty-two inches long, measuring from the tip of the nose to the root of the tail. It will weigh from eight to fifteen or more pounds, depending upon its size and condition. This animal belongs to a primitive order of mammals—the marsupials, a group that carry their nearly embryonic young in a special pouch outside the body. Only two species occur in the United States—the Virginia opossum, and the Texas opossum. However, a subspecies is found in Florida and over a restricted area in the extreme Southeastern part of the country.

This animal is omnivorous in its feeding habits, eating almost any available flesh food and many kinds of fruit. It frequently partakes of the carcasses of domestic or wild animals, and may often be found eating pawpaws, blackberries, wild grapes, apples, and persimmons. It is nocturnal in its prowlings, but travels øn moonlit nights as well as on dark nights. It has the peculiar habit of curling up motionless when approached, very much resembling a dead animal—"playing 'possum." It appears that the opossum has no special preference in regard to the type of country it inhabits, being found equally plentiful among the hills, in the woods, or on prairie land. However, it does not frequently invade swampy or marshy land, but is often found in wooded bottoms.

Where to Find Opossums

Opossums love to roam about in dense thickets, brier patches, hilly woodlands, old pastures, and around haystacks and straw-stacks. In wilderness sections, they often may be found around brier-choked slashings, on bush-grown hillsides, and at the edges of woods and dry arroyos.

Look for opossum tracks and signs in paths in neglected pastures and around old dilapidated farm buildings. Their dens are much like those of the skunk, and may often be found among the sprouts and briers on rocky hillsides or along bush-grown fence rows. Not infrequently this animal uses the dens of woodchucks and other animals. It is no trouble to recognize this animal's tracks, since the imprint of the hind foot plainly shows the "thumb," which sticks out at an angle from the foot.

Don't overlook the possibilities of hollow stumps and hollow logs when you are looking for the signs of this animal. Opossums use frequently about such places, as well as around brush heaps and log heaps. An old rail fence with its customary strip of sprouts and tangled vines and undergrowth seems to be specially liked by opossums, particularly if there happens to be a fruiting persimmon tree or two near by. The banks of dry ditches and the crevices around rock cliffs are good places to look for signs of this animal. However, one should remember that opossums are naturally woods' animals, and will more often be found in or near woods and thickets.

Best Methods of Trapping

The opossum is usually the young trapper's primer. Perhaps more beginning trappers try their hands first at trapping for opossums than for any other animal. The opossum may be easily caught in traps, is usually the most plentiful fur-bearer in its range, and can be captured with satisfactory success at bait sets, blind sets, den sets, or trail sets. It will often blunder into uncovered traps, and is readily lured to a set by the use of baits. Most youngsters, perhaps, trap it at its den; although this is not the best place to trap for it. Many opossums come to an untimely end at the hands of night hunters, especially in the southern half of its range.

Den trapping is hardly to be recommended, since there are other methods of taking the animal equally satisfactory and not so likely to cause alarm among the animals in a locality. Usually well-

Fence Sets—Good For Trapping Most Any Kind of Fur-bearing Animal. Trap at left set at an opening in the paling fence. Trap at right set in a runway beneath the fence. Traps should be set in shallow depressions in the ground, and both the trap and the drag should be well concealed.

worn trails may be found near dens; or maybe there will be passage-ways between logs, chunks, or beneath fences where traps may be set; or possibly there may be feeding grounds, such as fruiting persimmon trees, clumps of wild grapevines, or dense thickets, where one may readily trap the animals. Opossums are good climbers. They often explore old rotting or hollow snags. They also use much around dry drifts, and beneath haystacks. Paths in dense thickets and brier patches are good places to trap them. Try setting traps at the ends of hollow logs, at holes in the bases of hollow trees and hollow stumps, beneath old farm buildings, and at openings beneath fences. Such sets, of course, should be made only in territory where there are signs of the animal's presence.

The No. 1 and No. 1½ traps—or traps of corresponding size—are most suitable for trapping this animal. I find the underspring type of trap quite satisfactory, since it is small, compact, and may be easily set in narrow trails and openings. Whatever type of trap is used, it should always be fastened to a light drag; for this animal sometimes twists off a foot when captured in a trap with a fixed fastening. Always see that the trap is well covered, for one frequently catches mink, 'coon, or fox in traps that have been set for opossum.

Baits—How to Use

A great many opossums are captured in traps set at baits. The baits most commonly used in trapping the animal are the flesh baits and a few of the fruit baits. Flesh baits may be birds, rabbits, fowls, or the carcasses of wild animals or livestock. Putrid or partly decayed flesh of most any kind makes an excellent bait. Among the fruits, apples, persimmons, wild grapes, and pokeberries are good. However, fruit baits should be fresh.

Some trappers use artificial scents and lures in trapping the opossum. One popular lure for opossum consists of ¼ ounce of muskrat musk, ¼ ounce of beaver castor, 1 ounce of honey, 2 drops of anise, 1 grain of tonquin musk, and 4 ounces of fish oil. This latter item is used as the base ingredient. This lure is about as good as any for attracting opossums. However, in my own trapping, I depend mostly on natural baits.

Much depends upon placing the baits when trapping for the opossum. A partly decayed fowl placed at the end of a hollow log or among the crowded stems at the base of a clump of elders in a dense thicket will usually be found to be a very effective bait for this animal. Or a few ripe persimmons or half-eaten apples placed near the spot where several trails cross in thick underbrush often are effective. I have sometimes used small birds—sparrows or starlings—and rabbits to good advantage. But putrid baits will be found to be very good. Always see that the baits are half hidden by dry leaves or trash, and peg them down securely, so that they can not readily be dragged away. Choose a position for the bait that will force the animal to step in the trap to reach it.

Don't hang the bait above the trap, or place it on a stump, stake, log, or other object where the animal cannot easily reach it. Keep it on the ground, or at most only a few inches above the ground. Some trappers recommend dragging a piece of putrid meat through the woods and making bait sets along the trail thus made; but I have never found this a satisfactory method. It is a much better bet to place the baits in all manner of nooks and recesses along briery fence rows and at other suitable points in the woods and fields, partly hiding them to make them less conspicuous, so that they will not be disturbed by crows, owls, or other prowling depredators.

Judging the Worth of Opossum Skins

Opossums are always skinned so as to produce a cased pelt. The skins are stretched with the flesh side out. Skins should be thoroughly fleshed, so that there will be no fat left on the pelt. Don't overstretch opossum skins with the idea of making them larger, as this will detract from the value of the pelts.

Opossum skins are graded according to size, quality, and primeness. A prime skin is creamy white on the flesh side, has long, heavy fur with few guard hairs, and is weighty for its size. The best skins come from Northern sections. They are dark and heavy furred.

Opossum Tracks in Mud—Animal Walking.

Chapter XX

Beaver Trapping

The beaver is an animal of the streams, lakes, and ponds. It resembles the muskrat somewhat, both in appearance and habits, but is a much larger animal, often weighing from forty to fifty pounds. No doubt this animal had more to do with the early development of the raw fur industry in America than any other, since it was most sought after by the pioneer trappers everywhere. Beaver skins early became the standard commodity of exchange among the settlers. More than any other animal, the beaver was responsible for the influx of western migration, the incentive that caused the early trapper to pull civilization westward to the Pacific Coast.

Beavers are active animals, as may be inferred by remembering the old saying, "As busy as a beaver." Seen at a distance, they appear to be covered by rather coarse unattractive fur; but when examined at close range, it will be seen that beneath this outer coat there is a growth of beautiful, dark, glossy fur of fine texture and good quality. The animals have small front feet, but large sprawling hind feet, which are partly webbed. They have long chisel-like teeth, which enable them to cut down trees. The animals use their flat tails as rudders in swimming and as paddles with which to slap the surface of the water when giving their danger signals.

Formerly this animal was plentiful in all sections from Alaska and northern Canada to Mexico; but excessive early trapping so reduced its numbers and so cut its range that at one time it was in great danger of becoming extinct. However, as a result of closed seasons and restocking, the animal is now found in fair numbers in a great many sections throughout its natural range.

Being entirely vegetarian, the beaver subsists chiefly on the bark of twigs, branches, and the trunks of small trees. Occasionally it will partake of such articles of diet as flag root and succulent water grasses, but it greatly prefers such foods as the bark of poplar, birch, alder, cottonwood, and other soft woods, which it peels from poles and short sections of tree-trunks. These it cuts and floats to points near its dams and houses, where it anchors them beneath the water. It also uses the trunks and branches of saplings and small trees in building dams for raising the water level in streams, a work at which it is a past master, since it has been doing this for more than 25,000 years.

HABITS AND HAUNTS OF THE BEAVER

In early days, when this country was largely covered with timber, beavers built their dams and flooded the smaller streams throughout practically all parts of the country from Mexico northward. Now they are found only in restricted regions in northern and western United States, Alaska, and many provinces in Canada. Many of our finest and most fertile valley plains were created by silting from the flood waters caused by beaver dams—"beaver meadows," they are called. Such dams are usually small—a dozen feet through at the base, four or five feet high, and long enough to span a small stream. However, one was found in Estes Park in Colorada which was more than a thousand feet long!

Beavers are largely gregarious, living in colonies, like the muskrat. Their lodges or houses resembling overgrown muskrat houses made of sticks and poles, are commonly built in the water and have one or more underwater entrances, but sometimes they are erected on boggy land near water and have waterways reaching back to the stream or pond. There may be two or more apartments to the beaver's lodge. Often the animals use the lower room for storing food. Some beavers live in holes or underwater burrows in the banks of streams, much as do stream muskrats.

This animal is no great traveler. Once it is established on a stream or in a pond, it seldom moves out to new territory, unless it is unduly disturbed by too much trapping or by someone bungling his trapping. Not infrequently when there is a shortage of food and the animals locate a growth of cottonwood, alder, or poplar not too far from water they will make channels back to it, down which they can float the poles and billets of wood for storing in the vicinity of their lodges. They keep their dams well repaired at all times, trying to maintain an even water level about their houses. Being excellent swimmers and extremely strong in their necks and shoulders, the animals can manage heavy loads in the water, sometimes collecting and floating sticks or sections of tree trunks that would give a human being no little trouble to handle.

Beavers are never found far from water. They sometimes cross narrow stretches of forest to reach another lake or stream, but never wander around much on land. However, they often have regular runways near their dams and houses, over which they travel regularly. Not always will these runways be in evidence, for the animals may keep to the water in their activities and leave but little sign on land. In early fall, it is not unusual for them to travel a short way back from a stream or pond to reach some particularly choice food supply.

Where to Look for Beaver Signs and Tracks

Sometimes one may be able to arrive at a fair estimate of the number of beavers in a colony by examining carefully the dam and the shores of the flooded area in the vicinity of the lodges or houses. Although the beaver is a water animal, it does often get out on the shore to feed and play around at the edges of streams or ponds. Sometimes the animals have playgrounds where they puddle the muddy bottoms in the shallows or at the ankle-deep coves along the shores. Breaks or freshly repaired places in the dams are good places to look for signs of the animals.

Other good places to look for the tracks and signs of beaver are at points where the animals leave the water to reach a feeding ground at some alder or cottonwood growth back in the woods. Usually these places will be at low spots in the bank of a stream or pond. Too, one will do well to examine all small streams, for beavers not infrequently dam these and thus make suitable environments for their colonies. Where the streams have high banks, one may sometimes find the animals living in dens at the edges of the impounded waters. There may be houses with underwater entrances, where one may find places for traps. Don't forget to look for "workings" at shallow coves, and for trails and runways at the edge of the water.

MAKING SETS FOR BEAVER

One can usually find shallow places at or near beaver dams where sets can be made. Or one may often find very good set locations at places along the shore where the animals have been leaving the water. If one can find their playgrounds and set traps there at suitable locations, one will stand a good chance of making some catches.

Beavers may be captured in traps set at the openings to bank dens, much as in trapping muskrats. Feed bed sets are a good bet, too. Feed beds usually consist of cut brush and twigs that have been piled in small heaps in the water. They are often the twigs and small branches of willow, poplar, cottonwood, or other soft woods. Traps set about such places are fairly certain to catch beaver. One will often find hummocks rising above the surface of the water near beaver houses or at some little distance upstream from the dam. These are excellent locations for beaver sets.

A good many trappers use artificial scents in trapping for beavers. However, few such scents are efficacious in luring the animals. Perhaps the natural scent of the animal is best. Place this on twigs at hummocks, or at places along the shore where the animals have been using. Use natural scent rather sparingly. Beavers are wary. They will often leave a locality that is heavily trapped or that has been made obnoxious to them because trappers have been using too much artificial scent.

A ruse some trappers use to catch beaver is to cut holes in a beaver dam to cause leaks, so that traps can be set at them to catch the animals when they come to make repairs. This is a rather unsportsmanlike way of capturing the animals. It is not to be recommended. The method should be outlawed on general principles and such trapping is now illegal in many sections.

One should never use a trap smaller than the No. 3 for beaver. The No. 4 trap is much better for this purpose. The beaver is a powerful animal, and has sturdy sinewy legs and feet. It takes a strong trap to hold one. Always use a stout drowning wire when making sets for this animal. If the trap is located where a drowning wire cannot be used, fasten it to a seasoned hardwood drag. Otherwise the beaver is quite likely to chew the drag to chips and escape with the trap.

Skinning Beaver and Stretching the Skins

Beavers are skinned a little differently from most animals, since the job is done with the view of producing a perfectly round pelt when the skin is stretched. Work carefully with the skinning knife to separate the skin from the carcass, since the job will be largely knife work. If proper care is used, the skin may be removed practically clean of all flesh and fat.

Cut the skin around the forefeet and the hind feet just below the fur line. Cut around the tail at its base. Now make a cut from the center of the lower jaw down the center of the belly, and connect it with the cut made around the tail. Start skinning at the lower jaw, working the skin back both ways and being very careful not to cut or mutilate it. By doing considerable knife work, loosen the skin down each side of the neck and well back on the ribs. Do not slit the skin on the forelegs, but work it away from the flesh until the leg can be pulled through, like removing a finger from a glove. Do the same with the hind legs. After working the skin well down both sides, turn the carcass over and work the remainder of the skin free from the base of the tail and the back. Use a board surface or a hoop on which to stretch the skin, so that it will be nearly circular in shape when cured. It is often well to use ventilating strips on the board surface to prevent spoilage, especially if the animal's fur is wet or damp.

The skins of beaver are usually graded to size, condition, and primeness. Large, prime, well-furred skins from Northern sections bring the most money. Beaver pelts are seldom prime until in late winter. Early spring pelts are best. At this season, the fur is heavy and glossy, and of the finest texture.

Beaver Tracks—Animal Walking.

Chapter XXI

How to Trap the Otter

The otter is a water animal. It somewhat resembles the mink and the marten, except that it is much larger. A full-grown otter will weigh from thirty to forty pounds. It will measure around thirty-six to forty-eight inches from the tip of the nose to the tip of the tail. The body is plump and rather thick; the legs are short and stocky; and the bullet-shaped head sits squarely on the thick neck. Its ears are wide apart and so small that they are scarcely noticeable. Its toes are almost completely webbed, which makes the animal an excellent swimmer. Like the beaver, this animal has coarse guard hairs with an undercoat of thick, silky fur.

Otters are widely distributed throughout most of North America. They are great travelers at certain times of the year, but do most of their wandering by swimming in the waters of rivers, lakes, and ponds. In winter, they often swim under the ice, coming out at some air hole only to take to the water again at the next one. Because they love to catch trout and other game fish, they are frequently found around clear, cool streams. However, they will frequent almost any water where there are fish, crayfish, and frogs. This animal possesses an unusually well-developed sense of smell, and for this reason is seldom seen at close range. Unlike the marten, the otter will often be found in proximity to civilization, sometimes inhabiting streams and ponds that are constantly frequented by man. However, it is more commonly found in the wilder spots—back in the swamps and along the streams in thinly settled localities.

This animal homes in dens in the banks of streams and ponds. Usually these are at somewhat protected places—beneath the roots of trees, under drifts, or underneath overhanging vines or bushes. If there are steep banks near by, quite likely there will be an otter slide not far away. Here the otters spend much time in coasting down the slippery incline, much as children play at slides in parks. Too, the animals may have a playground not too far away at some deep cove or indented place along the shore, where trails and runways will be kept worn smooth by constant use. Like the mink, this animal loves to explore drifts and root wads. It will investigate every beaver dam within miles of its denning place.

Habits and Haunts of the Otter

Wooded swamps and clear, cool streams are the natural haunts of the otter, although the animal often may be found in almost any river, lake, or bayou where its food supply is plentiful. Not infrequently it may be seen swimming and playing around drifts or about logs in a stream or pond. It seldom is found very far from water, except when traveling from one stream to another. Unlike the beaver, this animal usually lives in pairs, or maybe sometimes in groups of three or four. But it never is found living in colonies.

The habits of the otter vary somewhat in different parts of the country. Therefore, in some sections, the animal may live and feed almost exclusively in the water, where it uses much about drifts or logs, while in other localities it may be found to be using more on the banks, or about coves and inlets.

In certain parts of the country, this animal apparently lives almost entirely on a fish diet; but in other places it may be found to be eating muskrat flesh, frogs, crayfish, and water snakes. Like the raccoon, the animal often hibernates during cold weather in midwinter, keeping to its dens in the banks of streams or ponds. But during the latter part of winter it is out again, traveling from stream to stream, or from pond to pond.

Otters love to use about the deep holes in rocky streams in the mountains, where there are many large boulders and an abundance of exposed tree roots along the banks. They are also frequently found along the rocky shores of lakes or ponds, or at almost any place where there are many drifts or tangled logs in the water. Lazy, crooked streams in the lowlands are good places for otters, especially if they are found in wooded territory.

METHODS USED IN TRAPPING THE OTTER

The otter is a sly, crafty animal. Catching it in a steel trap is not an easy job; and holding it after it is once caught is still more difficult, unless the capture is made near deep water where a drowning pole or wire can be used. Water sets are used almost exclusively although land sets are sometimes employed by experienced trappers who know the habits of the otter well.

Probably more otters are captured in sets where the animals leave the water near their slides than at any other set location. If one will examine the shore line carefully near a slide, one will nearly always be able to find where the animals emerge from the water to climb the bank. Set the trap here. Place it in two inches of water, cover it carefully, and fasten the chain to a stake out in deep water or to a drowning device of some sort. Make the set from a boat if possible, so as not to disturb the surroundings. But if the set must be made from the shore, use rubber boots and approach the location from the water. Never set a trap at the foot of an otter slide. It will only catch belly hair as the animal slides over it.

Sometimes trappers use the fence method of capturing the otter. Fences are made across small streams by staking with heavy sticks, leaving an opening at or near the center for the trap. This work should be done several weeks in advance of the trapping season, so that the animals will have become accustomed to using the openings before the traps are set. This sort of set is a good one, although it has the disadvantage of being apt to capture other animals that may be traveling the stream. Mink, raccoon, and beaver are particularly likely to be captured at such a set.

Many otters are trapped at abandoned beaver dams. Usually the traps are set at openings made in the dams. Many times otters have regular routes of travel where they cut across sharp bends or leave a stream to go to another near-by creek or river. These places are good locations for sets. Spring branches and places along the shores of streams where a jutting point or a rock or log forces the animal to take to the water are also good places for sets.

Occasionally trappers use bait sets for otters. Natural baits are most often used, such as fish or muskrat flesh. Old unused muskrat dens or shallow excavations in the banks of ponds or streams make the best locations for bait sets. One may occasionally find a hollow log or a root wad lying in the water, where good bait sets may be made. Although some trappers use artificial baits and lures in trapping this animal, I never have figured that they could be of any great advantage. A lure that is widely used by trappers in all parts of the country consists of beaver castor, otter musk, and fish oil. The fish oil is made by cutting small fish into tiny pieces, putting them in an uncorked glass bottle, then letting them hang in the hot sun until an oil is formed. Commercial fish oil is not so good.

Snow sets are sometimes used in trapping the otter. These may be made at various points along a stream or pond, at "cross-over" places where the animals travel from one stream to another, or at spots along the shore of a stream where shelving or overhanging banks make a narrow passageway. Perhaps the best location for snow sets is on the top of old beaver dams. Traps are sometimes set under the ice for taking the otter. They are usually placed at openings where the animals have been traveling. If it so happens that there is considerable space between the ice and the surface of the water at these places, baits may often be used to good advantage.

The No. 3 trap is the proper size for use in trapping the otter. Some trappers use a slightly larger trap, say the No. 3½ size, while others use traps as small as the No. 2½. However, the No. 3 trap will usually hold this animal under all ordinary circumstances, and will be found to be quite satisfactory when properly used. Otters have powerful legs and feet. For this reason, many trappers use traps with toothed jaws. Whatever kind of trap is used, one should keep in mind the fact that the otter's feet are set well to the sides of the animal's body and make allowance for this when placing the trap. Also, it should be remembered that the use of some sort of drowning device is necessary, since it is most desirable to drown the animal in the quickest possible time after it has been captured.

VALUING OTTER SKINS

Otter skins should be cased. Do not overstretch. Use a metal stretcher or a three-piece stretcher when possible, since the otter skins not infrequently shrink some in stretching and are sometimes most difficult to remove from a one-piece stretcher without injuring the pelt. Be careful in skinning the animal and in fleshing the skin. Always stretch the skins with the flesh side out.

The skins of this animal are valued according to primeness, size, and color. The large dark skins from Northern sections are the most valuable. Size, of course, also determines to no little extent the value of an otter skin. Like the beaver, the otter has a double coat of fur—a coarse outer coat and a fine, silky undercoat. This fur is not at its best until well along in the latter part of winter. It is then that the undercoat of fur becomes fine and silky.

Otter Tracks—Animal Walking.

Chapter XXII

Coyote and Wolf Trapping

Coyotes and wolves are closely related. In fact, the coyote is often called little wolf or barking wolf, although in appearance it more nearly resembles an overgrown fox. All wolves, however, belong to the family *Canidae,* which includes such animals as dogs, jackals, and foxes. There are several species in this country—some eight species and subspecies of coyotes and around nine species of wolves. Perhaps the best known of these are the common prairie coyote and the timber wolf or gray wolf. The range of wolves is wide, since they are found throughout western North America northward to the Arctic regions.

The coyote is the crow of the wolf tribe. Like this canny, devilish, black bird, he is wise, crafty, and playful. But he is very destructive, too. He is extremely clever in evading traps set for his capture. Much smaller than the timber wolf, he is no less destructive to young livestock. The coyote is often rather gaunt, and often presents a somewhat ragged and unkempt appearance. He usually sleeps in some burrow in the thick sagebrush or in a narrow crevice among the rocks during the day, coming out at night to hunt over the surrounding prairies. However, he may occasionally be seen in the daytime, usually skulking along the edge of some rocky canyon or slinking about in the dense undergrowth near the border of the desert.

During the summer, the coyote feeds chiefly on gophers, mice, rabbits, and ground-nesting birds and their eggs. But when the cold, snowy storms of winter bring a scarcity of these foods, the animal becomes bolder, often forming packs to prey upon the young of livestock. This animal has few enemies except man. Occasionally a young coyote will be killed by an eagle or a great horned owl. Timber wolves, too, sometimes kill the little ones. What has been said of the feeding habits and general characteristics of the coyote will apply in most part to wolves, except that wolves sometimes run down deer and other large animals in winter for food, while coyotes seldom attack large animals unless the animals are crippled or otherwise injured. Too, wolves not infrequently create greater havoc among livestock, particularly when the stock is out on open range.

Coyotes and wolves bring forth their young in the spring, usually in April or May. They give birth to litters of three to ten young. The baby animals behave much like domestic puppies during their first months of life. At this time it is not unusual to see them out, frolicking and playing about the entrance to the den. Young coyotes and wolves are fed by the parents until such time as they are able to hunt and kill for themselves. They develop a keen sight and a very acute sense of smell at an early age, and soon learn to catch crickets and small animals and birds. When they become a little older, they range farther from the home den, often following the parents on hunting trips. In summer, when food is commonly plentiful, coyotes and wolves frequently hunt alone, or in pairs, but in winter they often form hunting packs. Many are killed because of depredations among cattle and sheep.

HABITS AND HABITATS

Wolves have a touch of wildness in their nature that serves to keep them aloof from man and his activities. Although they sometimes visit man's corrals and ranches under cover of darkness, they seldom leave their haunts in the deep woods and sagebrush-choked arroyos in the daytime. Coyotes, however, may sometimes be seen near the habitations of man, not infrequently during daylight hours.

Occasionally they will come up near a rancher's home to play with the farm dog. But usually they, too, are rather wild and cautious. Ordinarily, they keep away from man and his abode, especially in the daytime.

Like the fox, the wolf and coyote use both their eyes and nose in hunting. They also use their ears to no little extent. Either animal can hear the rustle of quarry among the sagebrush at some little distance. Either can see and distinguish a man a long way off, or smell the scent of man or game at an unbelievable distance. Both animals are difficult to trap and hard to stalk, particularly if one is not careful about the way he goes about it. The constant efforts of stockmen and ranchers to kill off these depredators, together with the persistent hunting and trapping of the animals, have caused the coyote and the wolf to become educated in the ways of man. Therefore, these animals are much more difficult to hunt and trap today than they were a hundred years ago. They have well learned to associate the scent or sight of man with danger, and therefore give man and his activities a wide berth.

Coyotes and wolves are animals of the hinterland. They love the sagebrush-choked arroyos, the rocky canyons, the coulees, and the deep dark woods. Where the sagebrush is thickest and the shadows darkest, there is where the coyote or the wolf is found. Coming out at night to run on long hunts over the star-domed prairie or across miles of undulating range-land, or slinking along in the darkness down in a rocky canyon or stealthily hunting the rocky side of some tall mountain, the coyote and the wolf are at home in the wilds of the wildest West.

TRAPPING METHODS USED

In trapping coyotes and wolves, one has to consider individuality perhaps more than in trapping any other fur-bearing animal. There is no standard set that will take these animals regularly or with certainty. A set that will take one animal may be utterly useless in trapping for others of the same kind. Too, a set that works fine in one locality may be not at all successful in another locality. Or a set that catches the animals well this week may not be worth a whoop next week, even in the same locality. Each set must therefore be a law unto itself.

About the best advice one can give the coyote and wolf trapper is to study the tracks and signs of a particular animal and in this way become informed regarding that animal's quirks and peculiarities. Knowing something of the peculiar ways of the individual animal, he will then be in a much better position to make a set that will catch the animal. Devising a set that will meet the peculiar ways of a certain animal is a comparatively simple matter. Such a method of working is sometimes of very great advantage in trapping for any kind of bur-bearing animal.

Despite the fact that the individual coyote and wolf often reacts differently to any given set of circumstances or in any type of surroundings, there are some general methods of trapping these animals that the trapper may use to advantage almost anywhere. For instance, like the domestic dog, coyotes and wolves have certain bushes, snags, old bleached carcasses of animals, or clumps of grass along their regular routes of travel where they stop to urinate. Such places may be found by noticing the marks on the ground near by where the animals have scratched the soil after urinating. Traps carefully concealed at these places are fairly certain to make catches. If such places cannot be found, the trapper will do well to make some artificial ones along the animals' routes of travel. This may be done by sprinkling urine and natural scents of the animals on certain well-selected clusters of weeds, spears of grass, or low bushes near where coyotes and wolves are using. Well-concealed traps left at such places make excellent sets. Once a wolf or coyote travelway is located, several—but not too many—such sets can be made along the route of travel.

Old decayed and weathered carcasses of wild or domestic animals —or places where such carcasses have rotted away—make excellent places for setting traps for coyotes or wolves. These animals will often go some little distance out of their way to sniff or roll about such carcasses. Set the traps a few yards back from such places, leaving them near low bushes, clumps of weeds, or tussocks of grass. Always cover them with about half an inch of dry soil or sand, using a trap pad or other covering over the space inside the open trap jaws, so that dirt or other material will not get beneath the trap pan and clog the action of the trap. Other good locations for traps are at the old bedding grounds of sheep or cattle; at places where two or more trails cross; and at the most promising places at water holes on the open range. Narrow places in trails in rocky canyons or among the sagebrush make good set locations, as do also spots where a coyote or wolf has been trapped. Use scent judiciously, and only when needed to attract the animals from some little distance. Urine and the natural scent from the anal glands are best.

Baits are sometimes used in trapping coyotes and wolves. These should be natural baits—the carcass of a cow or sheep half hidden in sagebrush at the throat of a draw; a dead jack rabbit at the foot of a bush-fringed ledge of rock; the remains of a deer or other wild animal back in the bushes near a water hole; or a dead horse among the rocks at the head of a deep canyon. Sometimes a piece of partly decayed flesh buried just below the surface of the ground with traps set about it makes a very effective set. Bait sets are usually most successful, however, in those sections where natural foods are scarce or during times when there is snow on the ground.

The No. 3 and No. 4 traps are the sizes commonly used for trapping coyotes, while the No. 4 and No. 4½ sizes—or corresponding sizes—are suitable for trapping wolves. Be sure the traps are clean and free from foreign odor before setting them. Always wear leather or waterproofed canvas gloves when handling or setting coyote or wolf traps. Traps should be well concealed. Always see that the covering material fits in well with the surroundings. Be sure to place some sort of soft material beneath the pan of the trap, such as cotton, wool, shredded dry grass, or crumpled leaves. This will prevent dirt or trash from clogging the action of the trap. Fasten the trap to a drag of suitable size, which should be well hidden by covering with leaves or brush, or by burying in dirt or sand. It is well to shorten the trap chain so as to prevent any sudden jerks when the captured animal attempts to jump with the trap.

SKINNING AND STRETCHING

Coyotes and wolves should be skinned so as to produce cased pelts. Wolves, however, are often skinned to produce the open pelt, especially in certain sections in the West. But this is not necessary. Work carefully about the ears, eyes, nose, and mouth when skinning these animals. Use a sharp skinning knife, but use it sparingly. You will find it can often be used to advantage in skinning out the shanks, and in working about the neck and head. Always remove the bone from the tail.

Stretching coyote and wolf skins is a simple operation. The main thing to remember is not to overstretch the skin. Pull the skin just snugly tight over a suitable stretcher and tack it securely along the bottom. Do not attempt to get a big pelt by using a stretcher too large for the skin. Stretch the hide fur side out, as in stretching fox pelts.

Value of Coyote and Wolf Skins

Northern wolves have the most valuable pelts, the fur being longer and of darker color than that of wolves of more southerly regions. Like all other fur skins, coyote and wolf pelts increase in value with size, the larger skins being worth considerably more if the fur quality is good. The degree of primeness, too, largely governs the value of these pelts, as it does in other fur skins.

Bounties

In many parts of the country, bounties are paid on coyotes and wolves. Many trappers make considerable money by trapping these animals alone for bounty. Where the trapper is permitted to sell the pelts in addition to the bounty that is paid, the profits of trapping these animals are very worth while, especially in those sections where they are found in plenty.

Coyote Tracks—Animal Walking.

LYNX

BEAR

MARTEN

W. S. C.

Chapter XXIII

Trapping Other Fur-Bearers

Among the many fur-bearing animals are several that are of no great interest to the trapper. Some of these animals have good fur, but are too small to be of much value; others are so scattered over a large range or are found only in such limited numbers as to make the trapping of them unprofitable; while still others have fur of such poor quality that they are seldom trapped to any great extent. It has been thought best to deal with these animals here under one chapter heading, giving brief mention of each together with a few pertinent facts about trapping it.

FISHER

This animal belongs to the weasel family. It is a rather large fur-bearer, a full grown animal often measuring from thirty-four to thirty-eight inches from the tip of the nose to the tip of the tail. Its fur is dark, increasing in depth of color toward the rear part of the body. Its tail is dark and glossy, well shaped and rather bushy. Formerly this animal was found in fair numbers from the northern part of the United States northward. However, its numbers having been so reduced by persistent trapping and lack of suitable habitat, it is now found in sufficient plenty for profitable trapping only in a very few sections where conditions have been unusually favorable for its survival.

Fishers are trapped in much the same manner as mink or marten. Traps should be set in bush-covered or timbered country, usually along small streams or high on the summits of wooded mountains; for it is in such places that the animals love to wander in search of food. Baits—such as birds, rabbits, squirrels, mice, or fish—may be used; or traps can be set on logs that span a stream or lie with one end in the water. Many fishers are taken at cubbyhole sets made of chunks of wood or of stones.

Trappers commonly use the No. 2½ or No. 3 traps for trapping this animal. Being very powerful for its size, the fisher will often escape from smaller traps. Traps may be fastened by making use of the drowning pole or drowning wire when trapping near deep water; otherwise a clog or drag fastened to a long chain will be found of service. When sets are made among the thick bushes, two traps fastened to fixed objects and placed only a few inches apart will often make a capture more sure, since the trapped animal will not be so likely to tangle itself among the bushes and escape. Fishers should always be skinned so as to produce a cased pelt.

WOLVERINE

This carnivorous animal used to be found in fair numbers throughout northern United States and Canada, but is seldom seen now except in the wildest and most remote parts of its range. It is much larger than the fisher, sometimes weighing as much as ninety to one hundred pounds. It is a night prowler, and a most powerful animal for its size. However, it is a clumsy animal, and in general outline and habits greatly resembles a small bear. It lives in burrows, hollow logs, and in crevices in rocks. Its principal food is mice, rabbits, and such fur-bearing animals as it can capture. It seem to be especially fond of the flesh of the beaver and the otter. The animal is very scarce everywhere. How scarce may be surmised when one is told that the total number of wolverine skins collected even way back in 1902 was less than three thousand.

Perhaps most wolverines are captured in traps set about mink, marten, and fox sets that have been disturbed by the animal, since trappers seldom make a practice of trapping wolverines alone for their pelts. Being a great nuisance in springing traps and stealing baits intended for the capture of other fur game, this animal is considered an enemy to trappers everywhere and is speedily captured wherever found. Although the wolverine has the reputation of being uncanny and very elusive, trappers with whom I have talked say it is not so difficult to catch. They use a No. 3 or No. 4 steel trap, making sets often at baited cubbyholes. Sometimes they find the trails of the animal and set traps along these. Wolverines are skinned so as to produce an open pelt. The skins are handled much the same as those of the bear.

There are some five species of bears on this continent; the black bear, the cinnamon bear, the brown bear, the polar bear, and the grizzly bear. The black bear and the grizzly bear are the species of greatest interest to the trapper, since they are most widely distributed and are the ones most likely to be met with by those who go far back into the wild countries in search of fur game.

Bears are usually not dangerous animals. They will ordinarily keep their distance from man if not provoked or injured. They make their homes in rocky caverns, beneath shelving rock, under windfalls, and deep in tangled thickets and cane brakes. Their food consists of roots, berries, honey, fruits, insects, and fish. Bears sleep during cold weather in winter, coming out of their beds in early spring, often hungry and gaunt. Despite their awkward appearance, they are good runners, climbers, and swimmers. Their fur is dark and long, and is best in late winter and early spring.

This animal is usually trapped at bait sets. Large chunks of meat or the carcasses of wild animals are commonly used for bait. Honey is also sometimes used. These baits are frequently placed at the back part of a V-shaped enclosure made of logs or rocks. The traps are then set and carefully concealed at the open side. Clogs or drags of forty to eighty or ninety pounds in weight are used—forty pounds for traps set for the black bear; eighty to ninety pounds for traps set for the grizzly bear.

No. 5 traps are commonly used in trapping the black bear, while the heavier No. 6 trap is best suited to holding the powerful grizzly bear. These big traps are opened and set by making use of heavy clamps. Because of the possibility of accident, no one man should ever attempt to set these powerful traps without assistance.

MARTEN

The marten is a minklike animal of the dense forests and the stony ridges. It usually inhabits mountainous sections, frequently being found most plentiful in those wild, timbered areas that are seldom visited by man. Its range is from the northern part of the United States northward into Alaska. Its principal food is squirrels, although at times it also feeds upon small birds and animals. This animal is an excellent climber. Its toes are equipped with thin, sharp, curved claws which enable it to cling well to the branches and trunks of trees. The color of its fur is variable, ranging from a very dark color in the more Northern sections to a light brown in some sections farther South. The pelts of this animal are valuable, especially the dark pelts.

Bait sets are used almost exclusively in trapping for the marten. There are two types in general use—sets made on the ground and sets made on peg shelves on tree trunks or in notches cut in poles leaned against the trunks of trees. Most ground sets are made at the bases of hollow trees with the baits placed well back from the openings, or at baited cubby-pens made of pieces of wood or heavy bark. Sometimes a trapper places a bait so that it swings about three feet above the ground, then places and covers a trap carefully beneath it so that the animal will be caught when it jumps for the bait. Tree sets may be made by driving hardwood pegs into soft trees to form a shelf for the trap, then using baits fastened to the trunks of the trees about eighteen inches above the traps. Or a pole can be leaned against a tree trunk beneath a bait so placed, setting the trap in a notch cut in it at a point some two feet below its uppermost end. The No. 1 trap or the No. 1½ trap is commonly used in trapping this animal.

BADGER

The badger belongs to the bear family. It is about the size of a fox, but has a broad, flat body, short stubby tail, and short legs. It lives in burrows and underground dens, and subsists chiefly on roots, mice, birds, rabbits, birds' eggs, and the like. Its fur is long and thick, being interspersed with rather coarse guard-hairs. The pelts of this animal have a fair market value.

Badgers are powerful animals. It takes a strong trap to hold them. The No. 2 trap or the No. 3 trap should be used in trapping them. Traps should be set at the openings to their dens, somewhat within the entrance and a little to one side of the center. Inhabited dens may be known by the tracks and hairs about the openings. Use fairly heavy clogs or drags, fastening the trap chains securely to them. Badgers are skinned so as to produce open pelts.

WOODCHUCK

The woodchuck can hardly be classed as a fur-bearing animal, since its skin has but little commercial value and practically no fur value. It is often hunted and trapped as a pest, however, and is good for a bounty in some parts of the country. Its range is rather wide, comprising the northeast part of the United States and much of Canada. The hoary marmot in the Northwest and the rockchuck or yellow-bellied marmot of the Rocky Mountain region are close relatives.

Woodchucks live in underground dens, which they dig themselves, usually in fields, along neglected fence rows, or on rocky hillsides. They feed largely on clover and other grasses. The No. 1½ trap is used in trapping them. Sets are usually made at the den opening. Sometimes they are trapped by making sets in their runs near a den. This animal is skinned so as to produce an open skin.

MOLE

This common little fur-bearer is found in underground passageways throughout most sections in the eastern part of the United States. It has good fur, but is too small for its pelt to be of any great value. A larger species inhabits some of the Western states. In searching for food, this animal frequently makes underground tunnels that show a broken ridge of soil at the surface of the ground. These sometimes may be seen covering some little territory. Occasionally the animal burrows to the surface of the ground and throws up small mounds of fresh dirt. Its diet consists of crickets, grubs, roots, and the like.

Many types of mole traps are in use. These usually have a trigger arrangement that is sprung by the mole when passing along its tunnel. Moles are also often trapped in the No. 0 steel trap. An opening is made in the mole's underground passageway, where the trap is placed in position with its pan level with the bottom of the run. A piece of freshly cut sod is then placed over the opening.

Moles should be skinned so as to produce open pelts. The skins should be stretched on flat boards to dry. Trim off the tags and stretch so that the pelts will be nearly round.

RABBIT

The fur of the wild rabbit is not very valuable, since the animal's pelt brings but a few cents in the raw fur markets—scarcely enough to pay one for the effort of skinning the animal. Nevertheless, because of its use for bait in trapping such a wide variety of fur-bearers, the animal is of considerable interest to trappers everywhere. Too, in some parts of the country it is a pest, doing considerable damage to young orchards and gardens. It is for these reasons that it is being included among the fur-bearing animals of interest to trappers.

Trapping rabbits is easy. Traps can be set in the woods around freshly cut bushes or saplings, such as those of poplar, alder, sassafras, and the like. Too, trapping may be done in thickets, weed fields, or along brier-grown fence rows, setting the traps in rabbit paths or in the animal's runways. One can also set traps at dens, or at holes beneath haystacks. Many rabbits are taken in baited traps in thickets or brier patches. Corn, apple, or carrot makes a good bait.

The No. 1 trap is the right size for trapping rabbits. Heavier traps are likely to break the fragile bones of the foreleg, which not infrequently enables the animal to twist off a foot and escape. Fastening traps to very light drags will do much to prevent the escape of the captured animals.

CANADA LYNX

This animal belongs to the cat family. It is found in the wild mountainous sections of Canada, and in some of the wilder parts of northern and northwestern United States. A full grown animal measures around thirty-six to forty inches from the tip of the nose to the tip of the short tail, and will weigh from thirty-two to forty pounds. The animal uses in dense thickets and in the deep woods, often frequenting rocky canyons. It is usually found far from the settlements, away from civilization. Peculiarities of the animal are the single tuft of bristly black hairs at the tips of the ears, the thick bunch of long hair at either side of the head, just below the ears, and the stocky legs, big paws, and sharp claws.

The Canada lynx is a good climber. It does much of its feeding while climbing about lofty trees, catching birds and small animals. Too, it not infrequently pounces upon larger animals from some over-hanging limb or shelf of rock. It frequently stalks its prey, stealthily approaching its victims and catching them before they are aware of its presence. Being a night prowler, it is not often seen in the daytime.

The lynx is often trapped at baited cubby-pens. Small birds and animals are used for bait. The animal may sometimes be attracted to a set by the use of a few drops of fish oil on the bait. Scattering bird feathers about a set will also often attract the animal. The No. 2 and the No. 3 traps are frequently used in trapping this animal. The lynx is a powerful animal with big spreading paws. For this reason, many trappers prefer the heavier trap for taking it.

WILD CAT

The wild cat is found over a very wide range. There are several species, nearly all of which rather closely resemble the lynx in habits and general appearance. The animal measures some twenty-eight to thirty-two inches in length, not including the rather slender five-inch tail. It is a night-prowling animal, feeding largely on birds, rabbits, mice, rats, muskrats, squirrels, and the like. It lives around rocky cliffs in the deep woods, usually denning in hollow trees or in crevices among rocks.

Wild cats are trapped in much the same manner as the lynx. Any of the baits used for trapping the lynx will serve well in trapping this animal. Bait-cubbies may be used; or baits can often be placed in hollow logs or in crevices among rocks. Traps set in paths are often successful in taking the wild cat. Narrow places in trails about rocky cliffs are excellent set locations for taking this animal. Although many wild cats are caught in traps set for raccoons and mink, larger traps than are used for taking these animals will be found better for trapping wild cats. Usually the No. 2 trap is used. Some trappers prefer a little heavier trap.

BEAR -
FOREFOOT

LYNX

FISHER

MARTEN

BADGER

WOLVERINE

Animal Tracks.

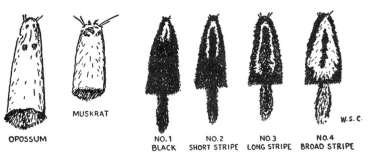

OPOSSUM

MUSKRAT

NO.1 BLACK   NO.2 SHORT STRIPE   NO.3 LONG STRIPE   NO.4 BROAD STRIPE

W.S.C.

SKUNK -
SKINS TURNED FUR SIDE OUT TO SHOW MARKINGS

Chapter XXIV

Care of Fur Skins

Nothing is of greater importance in trapping than the proper care of fur skins. The trapper who is uninformed about the correct way to skin his catch and to stretch and cure the skins, or one who is careless and sloppy about his work in the fur shed, may often lose many dollars that otherwise might find lodgment in his pockets. It is not unusual for the trapper who is careful in this work to make as much money in the fur room as he makes out on the trap line. To know how to skin a muskrat or a skunk so as to make the back side of the pelt longer is very worthwhile knowledge to any trapper. Or to know how to stretch a skin to the best advantage, or how to cure one properly, is just as important as to know how to set traps so that they will catch the most fur game.

Skinning—Open Skins—Cased Skins

To produce an open skin, make an incision with a sharp knife from the animal's chin down the center of the belly to the vent. If the animal has a furred tail, cut around the vent and extend this incision the full length on the underside of the tail. Otherwise, cut around the tail at the fur line and slit the skin back to the vent from the tail side. Now circle each leg at the ankle with the

143

knife, then slit the skin across the chest from one forefoot to the other and again across the lower part of the body from one hind foot to the other. Work the skin carefully from the body, using the skinning knife as little as possible. However, it will usually be found necessary to do some cutting about the neck and head. Use great care not to cut or otherwise mutilate the skin about the ears, eyes, nose, and lips. Skin out the tail if it is furred, being sure to remove all the bone, down to the very tip.

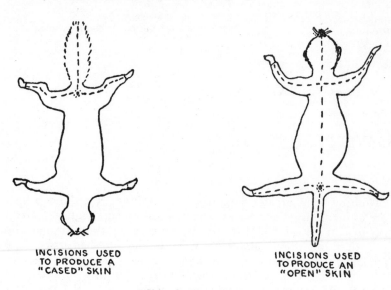

INCISIONS USED
TO PRODUCE A
"CASED" SKIN

INCISIONS USED
TO PRODUCE AN
"OPEN" SKIN

Skinning Fur Game.

The animals commonly skinned so as to produce the open pelt are the bear, badger, raccoon, wolverine, mole, woodchuck, and beaver. Wild goats and sheep as well as deer, and sometimes wolves and wild cats, are skinned to produce the open skin. Beavers are usually skinned a little differently to other animals, incisions only being made around the legs above the feet, around the tail at the fur line, and from the middle of the lower jaw down the center of the belly, across the vent, and connecting with the tail incision. The legs are not slit, as in most other animals.

All open skins are not stretched alike. Some are stretched nearly square; some are stretched to their natural shape; while others are stretched almost round. See under "Stretching" for information regarding the proper shape for stretching the skins of the different animals.

The animals that are skinned to produce the cased pelt are the wolf, wild cat, coyote, fox, muskrat, opossum, otter, fisher, marten, mink, weasel, and skunk. Rabbits are usually skinned to produce the cased skin also, although sometimes tame rabbits are skinned to produce the open skin, especially when the skin is to be used for rug work.

Skinning an animal to produce the cased skin requires care in making the proper incisions and having them in the right places. First, make an incision around all the legs at the ankles—unless the feet with the claws attached are to be skinned out, which is sometimes done when skinning the fox, lynx, fisher, weasel, and mink. Slit the skin on the back of the hind legs down to the vent. Cut around the vent and extend the incision the full length of the tail on the underside. If the tail is without fur, cut it off at the fur line. This applies to such animals as the opossum, muskrat, and beaver. Peel the skin from the body by pulling it away from the flesh, leaving the skin inside out. Some trappers split the tail only part way down, finishing the skinning by pulling the skin inside out over itself. But be sure to slit the skin to the tail tip later, as it is otherwise likely to spoil during warm spells. Use the skinning knife as little as possible, being very careful with it when working about the animal's head.

Sometimes when skinning an animal to produce a cased pelt it is desirable to have the back side of the skin to stretch to extra length and show all the fur possible. This is often the case with muskrat and skunk pelts. To accomplish this, make the leg incisions down the inside of the hind legs rather than along the back sides. Then in stretching the skin, pull it well down and tack it in a sort of semicircular fashion along the lower part of the stretcher. See that the tail is well centered.

STRETCHING—SIZE OF STRETCHERS

Stretching raw furs is an important part of a trapper's work. A little care in stretching pays big dividends later on when the skins go to the dealer's grading room. The main things about stretching skins to keep in mind are to see that every skin is properly centered on the stretching board—with the belly side on one side of the board and the back side on the other—and to be very careful to use a stretcher of proper size and not select one big enough to overstretch the skin. Pull the skin down snugly over the stretcher and fasten the lower edge evenly, so as to make a nice looking pelt. If working with an open skin, see that it is stretched well and evenly to the customary shape. Cut off all tags along the edges, and use plenty of nails or tacks to fasten the skin to the board.

Cased skins are stretched much alike, except that the hind legs of such skins as those of the fox, fisher, marten, wild cat, and wolf are pulled down along the edge of the stretching board and tacked to hold them in place. Open skins are stretched to different shapes. Raccoon skins are stretched nearly square, or, sometimes, a little wider at the tail end of the skin. Wild cat, wolverine, badger, and open wolf skins are stretched to their natural shapes. Beaver skins and mole skins are stretched nearly round.

Selecting the fur stretcher of proper size is important. Don't over-stretch a skin by using a fur stretcher too large for it. Have the skin fit the stretcher snugly, but not too tight. Elsewhere in this book will be found the proper sizes of fur stretchers for the various fur-bearing animals. It is always well to have several sizes for each animal on hand, so that a proper size selection can be made.

Curing Fur Skins

It is advisable to have a cool, airy place in which to cure raw furs. Never cure them in the sun or near a fire. A good circulation of air will keep out dampness, which is very detrimental to skins while in the process of curing. Dampness encourages molding; and molding is extremely bad for raw furs. The ideal place for curing raw furs is in a darkened, airy room, where there is an even, low temperature and a good circulation of air.

Fur skins should never be put on the stretchers while wet. Dry the fur by turning the skin fur side out and vigorously shaking it. Then hang it in the air a short while before stretching it. Don't, however, let it hang in the air so long that the flesh side begins to dry. It must be placed on the stretcher while the flesh side is yet "green"—soft and pliable. Wet skins are likely to mold before start-ing to cure. It takes about a week for the average sized skin to cure well; perhaps a little longer if temperatures are low.

Watch for blowflies among the curing pelts during warm spells in late autumn. They can soon ruin raw furs. They deposit their eggs on the skins. These eggs quickly hatch into maggots. Then one has a real problem on one's hands—and usually some spoiled pelts besides. Blowflies, however, are seldom a problem during cool, frosty weather. The best precaution against blowfly damage is to hang the skins in a very dark, cool place, where there is a good circulation of air.

Storing Raw Furs

The question is often asked if it pays to carry raw furs over to another season when they happen to be selling poorly toward the latter part of winter. This is usually not to be recommended—for two reasons. First, in some sections it is unlawful for one to have fur skins in one's possession during the summer. Second, raw furs deteriorate to a certain extent during warm weather unless they are kept in cold storage; and keeping them in cold storage is hardly feasible for the average trapper. Then, too, there is the danger of loss by vermin, fire, or from other sources. All things considered, it seems impracticable for the average trapper to attempt to store raw furs, at least for any appreciable length of time.

Chapter XXV

Marketing Raw Furs

To sell raw furs at home to a traveling buyer or to sell them to a dealer in some big raw fur center—these are problems that confront every trapper. Each method of selling has its good points and its drawbacks.

There is often a great deal of satisfaction in selling to the traveling buyer who visits one at one's own home. One gets to know such a buyer personally, becomes familiar with his way of grading raw furs, and knows what to expect in dealing with him when selling prime as well as off-color skins. On the other hand, one who sells to the dealer in the big city knows that he is doing business with a buyer who is only one or two steps from the manufacturer. He feels that he is overstepping the middleman and cutting out at least one or more profits between him and the consumer. Too, he feels that he will get good grading and full value—if he is certain of the dealer's honesty. For only by fair dealing can a fur concern nowadays grow big and prosperous.

The big raw fur centers are where the manufacturers' buyers come to buy the raw furs to be worked up into garments. Here is often where some of the large raw fur sales take place. It stands to reason, then, that the dealers near such places can, barring too much overhead expense, most nearly offer full value for the raw furs they handle.

Grading and Valuing Fur Skins

Whether a trapper sells his raw furs to a local dealer or ships them to some dealer in the city, he should always do his own grading and valuing before offering the skins for sale. It is a good idea always to have one's own estimates of the value of the pelts for comparison with those of the dealer.

Sort the skins according to size and kind, then examine each heap carefully for damaged or unprime skins. (Rarely one will catch an animal with an unprime pelt, even in midwinter.) Throw these in a heap to themselves. Now go through each heap carefully to determine quality in the pelts. Examine the fur closely, noticing length, color, thickness, silkiness, and luster. Look at the flesh side of the pelts. Are they smooth and free from all flesh and fat? Do they show that pinkish tinge of the prime pelt? Throw out all defective skins. These are to be looked over again later.

Now go through the heaps with a list of current raw fur prices handy for use in placing the correct value on the pelts. Try to determine as near as you can the exact value of each skin. Set down the results on paper. Don't, in your enthusiasm, put down valuations that are not justified by the quality of the pelts. It is imperative that you do this work conscientiously and as nearly correct as you can. By doing this, you will have your own valuation on your lot of raw furs to compare with the dealer's valuation, and, at the same time, be learning something of how to grade and value your own fur catches.

Packing for Shipment

The trapper who ships his fur skins to distant markets should know something about the proper manner of packaging his pelts. It is a good plan always to ship in one package when possible. Sometimes, however, the number of skins in a shipment makes it imperative that two or more packages be shipped. When such is the case, make note of the number of packages on each shipping tag. It is well to do this if only one package constitutes the shipment. Always place inside each package a shipping tag filled out with your name and address, the number of packages in the shipment, and the number and kinds of skins in the package. It is also a good idea to fasten two shipping tags to the outside of the package, for there is always the possibility that one may be torn off in transit.

When packaging the pelts, sort out each kind, wrap each pelt in paper, and tie the several kinds in separate bundles, always folding the tails in next to the fur and placing the skins so that the head end of one will be at the tail end of the one next to it. Wrap these separate packages together in burlap, affixing the shipping tags by tying them securely through the burlap and around the cord used in tying up the package. This can best be done by using a large needle and stout twine. Use stout cord for tying the burlap packages. Don't forget to place the inside shipping tag in the bundle before tying. See that your name and address appears clearly on each outside tag. Write a letter to the dealer in which is stated the number of packages being shipped, the number of pelts of each kind, and the method of shipping, whether by mail or by express. Also request that the shipment be held separate for your acceptance of the dealer's valuation, especially if you have not done business before with the dealer. Some fur skins can be shipped by parcel post, such as small shipments of clean opossum or muskrat skins. But large or medium sized shipments should always go by express. Such skins as those of the skunk, mink, and the larger fur-bearing animals should always be shipped by express.

SELECTING A MARKET

It is always something of a problem to decide on a market. There are quite a number of raw fur dealers advertising, each, of course, trying to get the trappers' raw furs. Some of the price lists sent out by dealers are gross overstatements of the current raw fur prices; others are conservative estimates of the current values of raw furs. Which dealers are reliable and dependable? This is the question of interest to every trapper who sends his fur catch abroad.

While there is no sure way of judging the integrity of a raw fur dealer by the claims he sets forth in his advertising, there are certain facts and "signs" that will enable a thoughtful trapper to form a pretty fair opinion of any buyer's methods of dealing with his customers. Don't patronize a dealer who puts out flashy, two- or three-color price lists with a sliding scale of extremely high prices. Chances are that he is a fly-by-night, here-today-and-gone-tomorrow dealer who is fishing only for one shipment from a trapper. He expects to "skin" a lot of trappers quickly, then get out of business pronto. Better pin your faith to the dealer who has been established in business a long time, and who puts out a plain, unadorned price list, stating clearly what he will pay for each kind and grade of raw furs. It is a fact that often the dealer who quotes the lowest prices is the one who pays most for raw furs.

Here are a few well-established fur buyers in different parts of the country.

S. Stanley Hawbaker & Sons, Fort Loudon, Pennsylvania; Ed Bauer Fur Company, Smithboro, Illinois; V. Saretsky & Company, Inc., 208 W. 29th Street, New York, N.Y. 10001; Massimo Fur House, P.O. Box 171, Harrison, New York 10528; New England Raw Fur Company, 1345 Newfield Street, Middletown, Connecticut 06457; R. L. Thomas, P.O. Box 61, Wadsworth, Ohio 44281. (Note: I hesitate to state which fur companies are best, since "best" is largely a matter of personal opinion. The companies I have named have been in business for years, and have thousands of satisfied customers.)

The best insurance against getting "stung" by a raw fur dealer is always to request that a shipment be held separate for the consignor's approval of the dealer's valuation. This, of course, necessitates a prompt reply on the part of the trapper, either accepting or rejecting the dealer's offer; for it stands to reason that the dealer cannot hold a shipment of raw furs indefinitely, awaiting the decision of the trapper.

Chapter XXVI

Tanning Skins

Trappers sometimes come into possession of fur skins they would like to tan and preserve. An unusually fine specimen of some beautiful or rare animal may be trapped; or a trapper may wish to give some special fur skin to a relative or friend, as a present; or one may wish to use some of one's trapped fur skins for making rugs, scarves, or gloves. In any such event, the knowledge of how to tan a fur skin will be useful.

PREPARING SKINS FOR TANNING

The first operation in tanning is to clean the skin thoroughly. If the skin is an old one, first soak it well in water until it softens. If the skin is a fresh one, cleaning can start at once. Wash all dirt from the fur, salt the flesh side well, then roll the skin in a tight bundle and let it lie tightly rolled from fifteen to forty-eight hours, depending upon the prevailing temperature. Now unroll the skin and scrape the flesh side well, using considerable pressure on the dull scraping knife in order to remove all flesh, fat, and muscle. Care should be used in this operation not to cut, tear, or otherwise mutilate the skin. After the flesh side of the skin has been prepared, wash the skin in gasoline, wring well, and hang it up until the gasoline has evaporated. This operation should be done in the open air, away from fire or flames. The skin is now ready for the tanning solution.

Tanning Methods

A very good method of tanning fur skins is as follows: Make up a quantity—a gallon for a skin the size of a fox skin—of a tanning liquor composed of water, salt, and commercial sulphuric acid. Use a gallon of water, bringing it to the boiling point, at which time dissolve in it a quart of common table salt, after which add one fluid ounce of the acid. Be careful in handling the undiluted acid. This forms the pickle or tanning solution. Allow the liquor to cool, then place the skin in it, stirring it about so that all parts will come in contact with the solution.

If the skin is the size of that of the fox, or smaller than this, leave it in the tanning solution from twenty-four to forty-eight hours. It should then be fully tanned. Larger skins may require a little more time to tan. A good way to tell when the skin is fully tanned is to remove it from the solution and stretch it first one way and then the other. If the flesh side of the skin whitens where the strain has been greatest, the skin is tanned.

When the skin has become fully tanned, remove it from the solution and rinse it well in a bucketful of lukewarm water in which has been stirred a handful of washing soda. Wring the skin out as dry as possible with the hands, then soak it for half an hour in benzine or gasoline, after which the fur is ready to clean. This may be accomplished by working the skin about in heated corn meal, then shaking the meal from the fur, repeating the operation until the fur is clean and bright. After cleaning in this manner, allow the skin to dry a little in the shade. Now soften it by stretching, pulling, and rubbing it in every part. This is a hard, laborious job; but there is no other way to make the skin soft, white, and pliable. Keep at this work until the skin is quite dry. Should some part of the skin appear to be drying too fast, such drying may be retarded by occasionally dampening the places slightly. If the dressed skin is wanted for rug purposes, moisten the flesh side and tack the skin fur side up on a flat surface, such as a board or a floor.

There are several types of tanning solutions. Another good one is made with water, salt, and pulverized oxalic acid. It is made by dissolving one quart of salt in two gallons of soft water, after which is added four ounces of the oxalic acid. This solution is a little slow in action, thus a little more time should be allowed for thorough tanning. Treatment of the skins is the same as when using the sulphuric acid solution, except that the rinsing may be done in clear, soft water.

Another method of tanning employs a tanning paste. This paste is made of aluminum sulphate, salt, terra japonica, and flour. Dissolve a pound of aluminum sulphate and one pound of table salt in a small quantity of water. Make another solution by dissolving two ounces of terra japonica in a little boiling water. Mix the two solutions, adding enough water to make two gallons of the liquid. Add flour to make a paste. Apply a coating of this paste to the flesh side of the prepared skin and roll the skin into a tight bundle. At the end of twenty-four hours, clean off the paste. When working with a heavy skin, it is frequently necessary to repeat the operation. When the paste has been well wiped off, rinse the skin in cold water. Wring dry, and apply a little vaseline or neat's foot oil, after which work the skin dry by drawing it over a taut rope or a smooth pole. Or it may be dried by stretching, pulling, and rubbing, as with the skins tanned by the other methods.

SECRET OF GOOD TANNING

The secret of good tanning lies not so much in the materials used as in the methods of doing the work. It is imperative that one remove all the native grease and oil from a skin before placing it in the tanning solution; otherwise a poor job of tanning will result. The retained native grease and oil will eventually cause the skin to become brittle and rotten. When the work of tanning has been well done, the skin will be as soft and pliable as velvet, and will remain that way permanently.

Chapter XXVII

Laws Affecting Trapping

Back in early days, there were no laws affecting trapping. Then, a trapper might trap when, where, and however he wished. He was largely a law unto himself. He could use deadfalls and snares, smoke animals out of their dens, cut den trees, dig out dens, set his traps anywhere at any season without license. In short, he could do just about as he pleased, with no law to say him nay. There was a general rule, however, that animals were sufficiently well furred to permit trapping in any month having an "r" in its name. This rule was observed by most of the old-time trappers. But such a rule was certainly no protection to fur game, since it permitted trapping over an extremely long season.

But later on, when the country became more settled, men began making laws to protect fur game at certain seasons. Regulations in regard to the kind of traps used in trapping and to the length of the trapping seasons were instituted. First, general regulations appeared; then, later on, we had laws applying to each State as well as to the entire United States. Later, licenses were required in most parts of the country to hunt, fish, and trap. Today both residents and nonresidents must procure a license before they can legally trap. These regulations apply in general to Canada, as well as to most United States' possessions.

GENERAL CONSIDERATIONS

Trappers will do well to remember that we now have National, State, and Provincial game and fish laws, which are subject to change from year to year. Many of these affect trapping. It is therefore advisable for trappers to familiarize themselves with existing laws before going afield to set traps anywhere. Certain fur-bearing animals are protected in nearly all parts of the country, and can be legally trapped only during specified periods, and then often only in restricted localities. Other animals are not protected at all, and may be legally trapped at any season. Still others are considered pests, and in some sections are often trapped for bounty. There are special laws, too, which often cover trapping regulations as well as the shipping of fur skins.

Since laws are constantly changing from year to year, enumeration of specific laws in a book of this kind would hardly be practicable. Therefore, it has been thought best to discuss herein only some pertinent facts regarding the laws that affect trapping and at the same time direct the trapper to sources of more specific information.

Copies of game laws may be had by applying to the state or provincial game officials of the States or Provinces where trapping is contemplated. Information regarding Federal laws may be had by writing the Secretary of the Interior, Washington 25, D. C.; or by writing the Director, Fish and Wildlife Service, Department of the Interior, Washington 25, D. C. A pamphlet giving laws and regulations relating to migratory birds and certain game mammals may be had by writing the Superintendent of Documents, U. S. Government Printing Office, Washington 25, D. C., enclosing ten cents in payment. This pamphlet gives a list of officials from whom copies of the game laws of the various States in the United States and the Provinces in Canada may be obtained.

Local Laws and Restrictions

Many of the States and Provinces have laws that affect trapping locally. Sometimes these limit the trapping of certain fur-bearing animals to specific parts of a State or Province. Certain trapping regulations may thus be different in adjoining localities. Bag limits or possession limits may thus sometimes vary in different parts of the same State or Province. License requirements are sometimes affected, too. Not infrequently the shipping of game or raw furs out of a country is affected by such local restrictions.

It is always well for the trapper to inform himself in regard to these local laws and restrictions before setting out traps, especially when operating in new territory. He may thus save himself no little trouble and possibly some rather heavy fines. It is much better to be informed than to become entangled in the law. For ignorance is no excuse in the eyes of the law. "I didn't know it was against the law" won't keep one from having to pay a fine.

Special Laws

Sometimes there are special laws. Perhaps some fur-bearing animal, such as the beaver or the otter, has been so closely trapped in certain sections or localities that it has become almost extinct there. In such circumstances, certain special laws are often brought into effect. These may apply only to specific sections. They may limit the trapping of the animal, or they may make the trapping of a certain animal or animals unlawful for a few years. Then we sometimes find laws that affect license fees or privileges in a given local territory. Bounties, too, are often governed by special laws —sometimes applying to a County, sometimes to a State or Province.

The laws in some parts of the country require the trapper to affix trap tags to his traps, each tag bearing his name and address. Other parts of the country do not have these laws. In some sections, it is unlawful to set traps at beaver dens, muskrat houses, or to place traps within the entrances to dens. Since these special laws vary so much in their specifications in various parts of the country, it is always well for the trapper in any section to inform himself in regard to what is legal and what is not legal before going out to put out his traps.

Index